Shorty!

**A Guide to Combating
Sexual Harassment
and Violence in
Public Schools and
on the Streets**

GIRLS FOR GENDER EQUITY

Joanne N. Smith,

Mandy Van Deven,

and Meghan Huppuch

THE FEMINIST PRESS
AT THE CITY UNIVERSITY OF NEW YORK
FEMINISTPRESS.ORG

Published in 2011 by the Feminist Press
at the City University of New York
The Graduate Center
365 Fifth Avenue, Suite 5406
New York, NY 10016

feministpress.org

This book is made possible in part by a grant from the Heller-Bernard Fund
of the Funding Exchange.

Second printing May 2012

Cover design by John Yates, steelworks.com
Text design by Drew Stevens

Library of Congress Cataloging-in-Publication Data

Hey, shorty! : a guide to combating sexual harassment and violence in public
schools and on the streets by girls for gender equity ; Joanne N. Smith, Mandy
Van Deven, and Meghan Huppuch.
    p. cm.
  Includes bibliographical references.
  ISBN 1-55861-669-1
1. Sexual harassment—United States—Prevention. 2. Sexual harassment of
women—United States—Prevention. 3. Sexual harassment—Study and teaching—
United States. I. Smith. Joanne N. II. Van Deven, Mandy. III. Huppuch, Meghan.
IV. Girls for Gender Equity.
  LC212.82.H49 2011
    371.5'8—dc22

                                                                        2010050135

Contents

Appendixes

Dedicated to the memory of Jeani Blalock
October 3, 1954–January 26, 2011

"When I dare to be powerful, to use my strength in the service of my vision, then it becomes less and less important whether I am afraid."
—Audre Lorde, *The Cancer Journals*

"Before being in Sisters in Strength, I never thought much about activism and organizing. After everything we've done together, I realize we all have a voice. To get together and speak out is how you can change a problematic situation."
—Nadia Jalil, youth organizer

Mission Statement

Girls for Gender Equity (GGE) is an intergenerational grassroots organization committed to the physical, psychological, social, and economic development of girls and women. Through education, organizing and physical fitness, GGE encourages communities to remove barriers and create opportunities for girls and women to live self-determined lives. A Brooklyn, New York-based coalition-building and youth development organization, GGE acts as a catalyst for change to improve gender and race relations and socioeconomic conditions for our most vulnerable youth and communities of color. Our work is a result of the many gracious and courageous allies to whom GGE is forever indebted.

Introduction
Joanne N. Smith

When I advocate for our most vulnerable girls and women at the intersection of gender, race, class, and sexual oppression, I'm advocating for myself and my family. In many ways, my childhood experiences shaped my professional aspirations and provided me with the vision to start GGE at the turn of the twenty-first century. My parents are Haitian immigrants who fled their country to escape the horror of a fourteen-year-long dictatorship by "Papa Doc" Duvalier, which claimed the lives of close to fifty thousand Haitians. I was born in Queens, New York, some years later, and grew up in Montgomery County, Maryland, with two amazing sisters, Natasha and Rachel, in a household led by our fearless mother, Irmone Leger. At a young age, I realized my passion for playing sports; soccer, basketball, and running cross-country provided a place for me to channel life's disappointments, pressures, and fears. Thankfully, multiple opportunities existed in Maryland at free, local recreation centers and on school teams. These opportunities may not have been created with a black Haitian girl in mind, but my mother took advantage of them. Athletics kept me in school, off the streets, and led me to college on basketball and academic scholarships.

After graduating from Bowie State University in 1997, I moved back to New York with the help of my cousin Guilaine. I worked as a case manager for two not-for-profit organizations serving families infected and affected by HIV/AIDS. I was committed to supporting all the children and families I was assigned to, but it was my unsuccessful search for an after-school program for Lilly, a twelve-year-old girl whose mother was living with AIDS, that led me to challenge the limited opportunities and outlets for girls living in urban communities.

The youngest of three children, Lilly lived in a three-bedroom town house in Coney Island with two older brothers and her mother. Lilly's father, an intravenous heroin abuser who had transmitted HIV to her mother eight years prior, left the home when Lilly was five. A great conversationalist, Lilly's mother was an intelligent, independent, and witty Latina woman. One afternoon during a home visit, while Lilly's mother cooked dinner in the kitchen, I sat on a stool at the island table, enjoying my talk with her and completing my paperwork. Lilly emerged from her room wearing long basketball shorts and high-top sneakers, palming her basketball in her left hand. Although I always saw various basketballs around the house, I had never associated them with Lilly until that moment.

Her mother stopped her midstride to ask, "Where you going?" While rolling her eyes Lilly spun the ball on her right index finger and answered, "Ma, where does it look like?" With a smile on my face, I chimed in, asking, "Lilly, are you a balla?" She checked my bluff, "I can take you!" Lilly stood around four feet nine on the outside, but clearly felt six feet tall on the inside. Instantly I knew I really liked this kid, and I jumped up from my seat. Stopping myself before attempting to tap the ball out of her hands as she protected it—playing b-ball in the house is a bad habit especially when it's not your house—I looked back at her mother, remembering why I was here. I was relieved to see her standing by the sink washing vegetables and looking at us with a smile on her face that said, "Sounds like a challenge to me." Thrilled, I packed up my work and with a thank-you head nod, I let her know that this would not take long.

Lilly led us to the backyard court where I was disappointed to find a square, plastic milk crate with the bottom cut out of it, screwed to a wooden board against her house, as the hoop. Without hesitation, Lilly dribbled around the ten-by-ten-foot cement court where trash cans lined the out-of-bounds mark so we wouldn't run into the wooden fence, and recycling bins represented how far we needed to take the ball back as we played twenty-one.

While we played, Lilly shared with me how well she did in school, her dreams of being a basketball player, and her desire to move far away from Coney Island where all she saw was drugs and gangs; there was nothing for her there. When I asked Lilly if we should talk to her school or local community center to start the program she wanted, she said, "Yeah right, not gonna happen. They don't see me or hear me; why would they create anything for me?" Her cynicism echoed truths about the powerlessness that girls feel when they merely survive the conditions they are presented, and feel unable to change systems they did not create, even to do something as simple as play sports. This gut-wrenching reality boiled my Haitian blood. I was "fortunate" to move from New York City to Maryland, to graduate from college magna cum laude and debt free. Yet, this same poverty-challenged, potential-filled, first-generation immigrant girl was me.

As the third born, I had learned how to fight, and had fought all my life. As long as girls everywhere felt that they had no choice but to accept their fate, I could not escape the multilayered oppression of race, class, and gender. Lilly's words planted a seed, awakening my dormant consciousness. That day I pledged: "In my lifetime, I will help to right many more of the social wrongs plaguing our most vulnerable. Today, I will create change for these forgotten girls."

I internalized this pledge and, without any real plan, confided in a close friend, Farah Tanis, cofounder and former executive director of a local organization committed to the rights of Haitian women and girls, called Dwa Fanm (meaning "women's rights" in Haitian Creole). She wholeheartedly supported my vision to develop programming that supported the optimal development of girls during their preadolescent years, a time when they have the highest level of self-esteem and are the most vulnerable. I would mobilize community members to change the systems that oppressed our most underserved and underutilized population—girls of color living in low-income communities. Farah recommended and helped me apply for the Open Society Foundation Community Fellowship. I thought this was absurd. I didn't know how to write a proposal; I hadn't gone to school for that. I didn't even like to write papers.

Farah pointed to all the ad hoc groups I had created for youth and survivors of domestic violence, my volunteer experience, and my passion for youth, sports, and justice. She reinforced this argument by saying, "You have nothing to lose. Just write about what you want to do with your life. Proposals are just another genre of writing, and I'll edit it with you." It's so important to have allies who at times believe in you more than you believe in yourself.

I completed a community needs assessment to garner feedback from girls and community members, and engage community support. Returning to my undergraduate psychology research books, I created focus group questions, surveys, and interview questions, then gathered answers by interviewing youth, adults, activists, parents, anyone who would give me a minute. I interviewed people attending district board meetings, spoke to parents at local PTA meetings, conducted ad hoc focus groups at local parks and recreation centers, and visited community-based organizations doing similar work to see if there was a need for another program. I talked to officers at police precincts regarding safety issues, and I researched online. I spoke with Michael J. Moon, Title IX coordinator at the New York State Education Department. He told me that sexual harassment and assault in the Bedford-Stuyvesant section of Brooklyn was actually being "perpetrated against girls as young as five years old." He stressed the urgency for this work, and sent me all the Title IX material he had on how to bring schools into compliance.

The process of applying for a grant forced me to create a thoughtful and thorough work plan, timeline, and organizing plan. As I worked on the needs assessment, I felt fueled and developed confidence in the project. When I interviewed girls I saw sitting on or playing in front of their stoops, I learned that many of them had been given adult responsibilities by the age of ten. Needed by their single mothers, they were responsible for picking up younger siblings from school, making sure they ate meals (which often consisted of cheap fast food) and making sure they did their homework. The top three needs voiced by most girls were for fun programming tailored specifically for them, opportunities to make money, and the ability to be outside whenever they wanted like the boys. Overall, they needed affirming programs to overcome poverty, and to create a safe community.

As part of my fellowship application, I needed letters of support from the community. Initially I was concerned that these might be difficult to get, so I was amazed when most, if not all, the people I reached out to were willing to write a letter on my behalf. I was even confronted by people who wondered why I hadn't asked them to sign a letter, so I did. With that spirit, I received eighty signatures on a letter petitioning the Open Society Foundation to support the launch of an organization for girls in 2001.

The needs voiced by the girls themselves led me to focus on youth-centered programming and community organizing. Under the auspices of Title IX of the Education Amendment, the organization would lead campaigns to fight against gender inequity and dispel the belief that girls should be seen only as little adults, future mothers, sexual conquests, baby mamas, or wives. It would be a space where girls of color would be treated according to their youth development stage, and they would be supported as young people whose play was their work.

Our program was due to begin at the Bedford-Stuyvesant YMCA on the afternoon of September 11, 2001. Like people all over the country, I woke to witness thousands of lives being tragically changed that morning. Feeling shocked, confused, helpless, and scared, I tried to reach my cousin Guilaine, a sergeant with the New York City Police Department, but couldn't get through because cell phones weren't working. I wasn't sure if I should go to the Y as scheduled at three o'clock that afternoon. But then I thought that if girls were waiting for me, I had better show up. It was the best decision I ever made. The girls needed something positive to focus on that day, and so did I.

Girls for Gender Equity (GGE) was born that afternoon with a mission to bring about social change by promoting sports and educational opportunities for girls aged seven to twelve. GGE would promote girls' overall empowerment, including access to health care and safety on the streets of our underserved communities in central Brooklyn.

After several meetings, I was confused when some of the girls did not change into gym clothes as we gathered in the gymnasium. I took an eleven-year-old girl aside to ask her why she wouldn't run full speed, or try harder to get the ball. It took a few of these one-on-one discussions to break through her tough exterior and excuses. Finally, she revealed how uncomfortable she felt about her lack of bra support and how the boys on the sideline looked at and talked about the girls' bodies when we played. Clearing the gym of all male spectators before practices and group meetings became standard practice.

As an avid basketball player having played with and against boys and men since age ten, I had repeatedly witnessed, and personally experienced, blatant sexual harassment, gender-based discrimination, and threats from men. I suddenly realized how many times I had brushed off being sexually harassed as incidental contact because everyone knows "boxing someone out" requires you to put your butt on them or "setting a pick" means preparing for the chest-to-chest impact your breasts will receive. I became angry as I recalled the countless times I had silently believed I was being accepted as an athlete while being groped. As a result of these experiences, it was encouraging to see Anasia, a seven-year-old with a light-brown complexion, slim body, bright, black marble eyes, and a vibrant smile, zealously accept her leadership role in clearing the gym of boys and men when it was our time to play. She'd project her voice and sometimes use the bullhorn to announce, "All right boys, pack it up. It's four o'clock and this is our space now. Please get dressed downstairs in the locker room."

The boys and men ignored her at first, but before I could take over, Mr. Al Vann, a neatly dressed, older black gentleman whom I had never met but often saw coaching local, elite players, and whose daughter was an exceptional player at Duke University, stopped his instruction and shouted, "You heard them, pack it up."

The men and boys alike did just that and followed him out of the gym as we all high-fived Anasia for clearing the gym and proceeded to set up. Clearly, Mr. Vann was an ally; he worked with GGE for many years and deserved every bit of respect he was given. Soon the mere sight of Anasia had the boys and men clearing the courts. Everything was working as planned; the Y supported our initiatives while we helped to boost their enrollment of girls under twelve years old.

Canvassing bulletin boards at the neighborhood grocery stores, churches, and college brought local schools, women, high school students, and youth to us. In two short months we recruited fifty-five girls and eight women coaches as volunteers. Everyone, including parents, responded well to all our programming and events. Having created a space where our girls were blossoming, we felt proud of the work we were doing.

Unfortunately, this feeling of progress was halted suddenly in December 2001. An eight-year-old girl was walking to her local elementary school at eight in the morning, and noticed a man following her. She began to walk faster, but he increased his speed as well. She remembered passing a couple of corner stores, but did not go inside. When she was later questioned by police she said she didn't want to be embarrassed, and she was only a block away from school. She didn't feel right about the situation, but she thought that if she slowed down and allowed the man to pass, he would continue on. She slowed down, and the man, smelling of alcohol and wearing red contact lenses, grabbed her and dragged her to a nearby rooftop where he brutally raped her, then fled. She managed to make it to the school before collapsing into the principal's arms, eventually gathering enough strength to report the rape.

This eight-year-old child attended the same local elementary school that many of our girls attended. As program participants met me in the gym that afternoon, they raced to blurt out the details of this traumatic experience. I was shocked. It was so painful to hear that a child had been raped, and that it had happened only five hundred feet away from where we lived, played, and worked. The girls and I wondered whether to discuss the incident and the girls' reactions to it in place of practice. With a unanimous vote we sat around the half-court circle to share our feelings.

The girls repeated comments that they had heard from teachers, parents, and other youth: "She deserved it," "She was fast," "She shouldn't have been alone." I was stunned and angry, confronted by the reality that society trains girls to internalize misogyny. Blaming the victim by identifying with the aggressor allowed the girls to distance themselves from her, thereby creating a false sense of security. The fact that the child was able to walk to school, bleeding and crying after being raped, without anyone stopping her to ask, "What's wrong?" or "Are you okay?" told our girls that people had no compassion for abused black girls. It also communicated to our girls that if they were seen as weak or vulnerable, they were powerless against an attack. Although the victim looked like them, went to their same school, and did the same things they did daily, she must have done something wrong to bring this on herself.

In that circle, I pressed the girls to hear themselves, and to see that the man's role as a rapist, who had committed a violent crime against a child, was not being acknowledged. After an hour and fifteen minutes, a child, her voice full of conviction, said, "That's why she shouldn't be fast, wearing them clothes, act like a woman be treated like a woman." Having never dealt with an incident like this, and being caught totally unprepared, I handled the situation badly by ending the conversation with a disapproving fifteen-minute speech countering every one of their points. Then I sent the girls home.

That night I felt defeated. I confronted an extremely difficult question: Could GGE really effect change? All I could think about was how this eight-year-old baby had walked to school bleeding and disheveled without anyone asking her if she needed help. She was only visible to the man who wanted to rape her. A puppy roaming the streets would never have gone unnoticed if it were bleeding. This rape received little media coverage or community response. Many adults in the neighborhood did not know about it until I told them. The facts of this rape, and the lack of community response, were my gut check: doing nothing was not an option.

I founded GGE at the same time that I was accepted into Hunter College School of Social Work. I utilized my support systems in the school as well as those in my personal life: peers, professors, my supervisor, my therapist, and friends. (Did I mention that allies are golden?) With only eight volunteers and no board of

First Annual Mother Daughter Health and Play Day, 2001. Anasia, kneeling in the center in pigtails.

directors, I organized a group of girls to march through the streets of Bedford-Stuyvesant in protest of the rape. The Guardian Angels, a volunteer street patrol, were present since they felt that the police weren't doing anything, and their demands led to a town hall meeting with the police, the school, and parents. With the support of then GGE board member Madeline Curren, we began to make *Our Girls Time*, a monthly newsletter to revolutionize the way the community saw women and girls.

To bring the community together, GGE hosted our first annual Mother Daughter Health and Play Day (MDHPD) at the Bedford Y. Comments heard from daughters included, "I didn't know you could do that," or "I didn't know you could run so fast." Mothers said, "I've never played like this with her," and "GGE should have this day just for mothers, without the kids." From the way that mothers dove over their daughters for a loose ball, and tackled other collegiate athletes to win a race, all while laughing, MDHPD made it clear that women needed a place to play, compete, and take care of their needs as active people.

With the girls, I began conducting Gender Respect Groups in between practices, using notes and activities created for a career day I participated in at Public School (PS) 56. During our group meetings, I asked the girls simple questions: "What was the first toy you ever had as a baby?" "What was the first toy your brother had?" "Let's list some characteristics of girls on one side of the chart and characteristics of boys on the other." The girls spewed stereotypical, derogatory answers about girls as I scrambled to write them all down. I thought to myself, "How in the world am I going to deconstruct these stereotypes? Where do I even start?" When I turned to question them about their answers, they were looking at the board as well, and to my surprise they interjected with comments like "Nuh-uh, girls ain't weak," and "That's not true, Ms. Joanne.

Kayla, Joanne, Agnes, and Veronica at the Gender Equality Festival, 2008.

Boys do cry," and "Write 'brave' under girls too. I am brave." As we crossed words out and drew lines to connect common themes girls and boys share, this opened the dialogue for us to share where these beliefs come from, how and why we reinforce them, and why we are expected to live up to them even when we know the truth about girls.

In the months to come, as we processed the spectrum of violence against women and girls, the youth found a place to empathize with their peers who had survived rape, incest, and sexual assault. This state of raised consciousness created a space for the voices of these girls of color to be heard and validated. As we shared fears, their responsiveness and openness demonstrated that their awareness was growing through our conversations. At their own pace, they came to terms with the fact that the man who had raped their classmate was at fault, and the eight-year-old girl, who could have been our sister, mother, aunt, or any of us, had done everything right. We had heard that she was moving down south because she was severely depressed and felt stigmatized, and that the family thought it was best. To show their support for her and her family, the girls made original cards, artwork, and brought in one personal item that meant strength or survival. We created a basket of gifts that I took to the school so the principal could deliver them, since the victim's identity was concealed.

By this time, Title IX was under attack. The Bush administration was not committed to enforcing Title IX policies and was actively looking to alter the law. The US Department of Education attacked the three-prong test developed for schools to determine their compliance with the legislation. GGE led a call to action, petitioning the community to join our task force to help save Title IX. To get the parents involved, we enlisted the help of Terri Clark, program coordinator of New York City College of Technology's Health Education Services and GGE board member. Terri led health workshops that addressed the high rates of breast cancer, hypertension, obesity, and diabetes that affect our communities, and stressed the urgent, preventive measures we needed to take. Creating the link between women's health and physical activity was important so that parents would understand the importance of Title IX programs in their daughters' lives. It worked. GGE, supported by the Feminist Majority and the Women's Sports Foundation, collected one thousand signatures and letters from activists, school officials, community members, and community-based organizations and sent them in a mass mailing and letter-writing campaign to Washington. The Department of Education announced that it would not act on any of the recommendations made that would have weakened Title IX.

In 2001, the Open Society Foundation awarded me the community activist fellowship. By summer of 2002, it was clear that GGE would become a not-for-profit. I applied for 501(c)(3) status, submitted funding requests, and recruited local women from the community as our founding board of directors.

Today, GGE is very much a work in progress. As an organization, we continue to learn from each other and understand that social change is lifelong work. Within this book, we share GGE's most painful stories, humble beginnings, and movement-building strategies as a gift of hope, strength, and inspiration. In just ten short years, GGE has mobilized thousands of community members and affected the lives of over five thousand youth and counting. Right now, our society is recognizing that gender-based violence is a health, education, and economic-development issue that negatively affects the whole society. There is much work to be done. And now is the time.

A Note from the Authors

Anyone who has ever been part of a group project can tell you coalition work ain't easy. You have to negotiate dissimilar personalities, time constraints, competing interests, and differing opinions about the best way to move forward. In the case of this book, we had the added challenge of one of our author's living on the other side of the globe. But the rapport we'd developed after years of working side by side made writing *Hey, Shorty!* as a collaborative team an enormously enjoyable experience. Founder and executive director Joanne N. Smith, former associate director Mandy Van Deven, and director of community organizing Meghan Huppuch all had a hand in bringing GGE's grassroots-organizing model into these pages. Other sections offer different voices, like Sarah Zeller-Berkman, PhD, participatory action research facilitator and founding member of the Public Science Project at the CUNY Graduate Center, and the teen women organizers in our Sisters in Strength program. As a result, there are shifts in the book's narrative, because, like in a rap battle, we were continually passing the mic to share our personal perspectives on GGE's mission to address sexual harassment in schools and on the streets.

We hope that *Hey, Shorty!* will be read by everyone who shares our belief that public schools should be safe for all children, that parents should feel good about sending their kids to school each day, and that all teachers should feel supported by their immediate supervisors and citywide leaders. This book is designed to be an informative tool for other youth organizers, students, parents, teachers, and allies who work within the schools trying to make them safer. It can be used by students to connect with adults in their schools, build power with their classmates, and create lasting change. Activists and educators of all ages can use this book to learn about meaningful ways to engage with and empower youth.

While this book documents GGE's development of a language with which to speak about sexual harassment and strategies to address gender-based violence in the New York City public schools, we hope that by sharing our experiences, we can provide guidance to all people eager to make any necessary changes within their own communities. Although your organizing issues may vary from ours, we hope you take away our overall message that youth should be at the forefront of advocating for their rights, and should be valued as experts about their experiences. Collectively, we have the power to enforce social change.

Title IX

No person in the United States shall, on the basis of sex, be excluded from participation in, be denied the benefits of, or be subjected to discrimination under any education program or activity receiving Federal financial assistance.

—Title IX of the Education Amendments of 1972
to the Civil Rights Act of 1964

GGE's work to eliminate gender-based violence within school systems is based on Title IX, the civil rights law requiring that any educational establishment receiving funds from the national government provide equal opportunities to students, regardless of gender. Through several legal decisions since 1972 it has been determined that Title IX covers the following ten key points*: access to higher education, athletics, career education, education for pregnant and parenting students, employment, learning environment, math and science, sexual harassment, and standardized testing and technology.

The passage of Title IX was a promising sign in the fight for girls' and women's rights, but poor enforcement has limited its effectiveness. Despite this civil rights law, many educational environments continue to be unfair, unwelcoming, and unsafe for all students.

Sexual harassment is one of the points of Title IX that is often overlooked. Title IX defines sexual harassment in two ways. Quid pro quo (Latin for "this for that") harassment is when a teacher or school employee offers a student something (like a good grade or a recommendation) in exchange for sexual

*The Ten Key Points as defined by the National Women's Law Center, "History of Title IX," www.titleix.info/History/History-Overview.aspx.

favors. It could also be a threat to lower a grade or treat the student worse than other students if he or she refuses to engage in a sexual act. Hostile environment harassment occurs when students, teachers, or staff at the school touch a student in a sexual way, make sexual comments, gestures, or jokes, or show sexual pictures. Hostile environment harassment is discrimination under Title IX if it is severe, pervasive, and objectively offensive, and if it bars the victim's access to an educational opportunity or benefit.

Title IX *requires* schools to take the following steps to help prevent and address harassment:

— Create and distribute a policy on sexual harassment
— Adopt and publish grievance procedures for complaints of sexual harassment
— Appoint one employee as the Title IX coordinator who will handle complaints of sexual harassment
— Respond promptly and effectively to reports of sexual harassment

Sisters in Strength
Mandy Van Deven

When I look back at my first year at GGE, I have to laugh at my naïveté. Upon accepting the part-time community organizer position, I had no idea that the New York City public school system was the largest in the country, nor did I understand its multilayered and complex manner of functioning. In hindsight, despite several years of prior activism, the 2003–2004 academic year was the year I cut my teeth as a grassroots organizer.

My first task at GGE was to further develop the Gender Respect Group into a curriculum, as a series of workshops intended to help girls and boys in elementary and middle school understand gender equality in an educational setting. Having never written a curriculum before, I looked for assistance to the numerous printed resources that Joanne and I had amassed from personal connections and online searches. (Community Organizing Rule #1: if what you need already exists, don't waste time reinventing the wheel.) Unfortunately, I could find no wheels (at least none that were affordable and age-appropriate), so I had to fashion one myself. The result was the Gender Respect Workshop Series: six hour-long sessions covering Title IX, the difference between sex and gender, stereotypes, discrimination, and sexual harassment.

I was a bit nervous about approaching the principals of the schools at which GGE provided Health and Fitness programming to pitch the Gender Respect Workshop Series, but it quickly became apparent that the administrators and staff were more than happy to accommodate any program—particularly one being provided at no cost—that might enhance their school's educational environment and boost student achievement. Testing is a priority in low-performing schools, and so long as the Gender Respect Workshop Series didn't interfere with or lower test results, GGE was golden. I arranged the series in a way that suited teachers' class schedules, provided all necessary materials myself, and started facilitating the workshops that would later get me dubbed both "the gender lady" and "Ms. V."

Mandy leading a Gender Respect Workshop.

Straightaway sexual harassment was the most controversial and lively topic in the series. Discussions of

stereotypes and discrimination are common enough to children in low-income neighborhoods where people of color, particularly children of Caribbean and African immigrants, reside, so talking about how prejudice based on gender is hurtful and should be avoided was not exactly new or groundbreaking information for the youth. However, in classrooms that were typically a little rowdy, conversations about "booty tag" (a so-called game boys would play at recess where they would grab girls' behinds), why no means no, same-sex sexual harassment, and queer bashing were tricky not only in subject matter, but in behavior management as well. Sexual harassment evoked strong emotions from girls and boys. It also elicited numerous disclosures about incidents that had happened in their schools. Everyone had a story (or two or three) to tell or a question that just *had* to be asked, and each student would fill up with excitement or nervous anticipation then burst at the seams when they got their chance to speak.

> At the time I started I wouldn't have considered it to be sexual harassment. It's this thing that happens to you because you're a girl. Catcalls, guys trying to grab your hand, trying to get from point A to point B. Shocked that these girls were naming it as sexual harassment, I felt confused and lost and wanted to understand it.
> —Kayla, youth organizer

After the workshops, teachers would confess their own experiences with sexual harassment to me. From hearing "faggot" in the hallways daily to having a ten-year-old male student make sexual overtures to a female teacher well into her forties, the most common response to the workshops from teachers was relief. They hadn't been adequately trained in how to have these types of conversations with students, and felt they were necessary in order for the high number of incidents they witnessed to decrease. On the other hand, the workshops also made some teachers nervous. While they knew the value of the information being shared, it was their job on the line if a misunderstanding occurred between the time the workshop took place and the time the child got home to tell their caregiver what they'd learned in school that day. If a misinterpretation did take place, the teachers weren't confident that they would be supported by their principal or the New York City Department of Education (NYCDOE).

The teachers' fears were heightened by my inability, despite an overwhelming amount of effort, to identify the Title IX coordinator for the schools in Region 8, the district in which we worked, for an entire year. In a conversation with then-Title IX coordinator for the New York State Education Department, Michael J. Moon, I was told that each district delineated by the NYCDOE was to be assigned its own Title IX coordinator: a person to handle any complaints issued for lack of adherence to laws governing gender equity in education. After numerous phone conversations with staff people throughout the NYCDOE, I was put in touch with a woman named Vera Evans* who agreed to meet with me at GGE's office.

Having played sports herself, Evans was a big supporter of girls' sports programs and was happy to talk to me about GGE's work, though she had never heard of Title IX. I gave her a brief history lesson on the pas-

*Names have been changed where we felt someone might feel unfairly singled out for their failure to enforce Title IX. We recognize this as a systemic failure and do not assign individual responsibility to the parties involved.

sage of Title IX and its impact on girls' and women's education. By the end of the meeting she assured me that she would identify the Title IX coordinator in GGE's region so that our organizing work would no longer be hindered. I left the meeting feeling refreshed: finally, a year's worth of phone calls had paid off—or so I thought.

After our meeting, Ms. Evans disappeared. She no longer took my phone calls or answered my emails. I even went to her office in person, but was told that she was in a meeting and that I shouldn't wait. Months went by with no contact from her whatsoever despite my repeated attempts. I was perplexed until one day an email appeared in my inbox that made the reason for her disappearance clear. The email read: "I am the Title IX coordinator for your district." It was from Vera Evans. The same woman who had never heard of Title IX before setting foot into GGE's office was now assigned the duties of making sure the policy was enforced? Despite my continued effort to get ahold of her, I never saw or heard from Vera Evans again. It was time to come up with a new plan of action.

While the gender respect workshops for children were taking place during school hours, GGE held workshops for caregivers after school to garner interest in being a part of our Title IX Task Force, a group of parents and teachers who would lead the community organizing efforts facilitated by GGE. Anyone working in underserved neighborhoods can tell you how challenging it is for caregivers to find the time to participate in extraneous school-related activities. Barriers to participation include working multiple jobs or jobs with evening hours, familial responsibilities, disabilities, and health issues—all of which take priority. By the end of the 2003–2004 school year, there were enough caregivers and teachers participating in the Title IX Task Force to complete the federally derived Title IX compliance checklist, which none of the school administrators had ever heard of, despite it being mandated to be completed on an annual basis. (The Title IX coordinator was supposed to be in charge of implementing the annual completion of this checklist in each school.) As the need to address sexual harassment had been asserted at all levels—by students, teachers, and care-

Sexual harassment is any unwanted physical or verbal contact. It is a silent word that lingers and spreads through your mind. You are ashamed. You can't focus. You want to speak, but you can't. Your voice is trapped in a small, locked box. You are suppressed by your fear, and you can't find help. You continue to be harassed. Worst of all, sexual harassment is as common in school as it is on the streets. It's unbelievable to see how often it happens day after day without students even realizing what it is. You question whether what just happened was right or wrong. As the teacher lectures on physics, your mind is elsewhere . . . probably blaming yourself for letting things happen and having no control. You don't know that you're the victim of sexual harassment. You hear this phrase so many times but live oblivious to it. It's complicated. School is not just a place to gain knowledge but also a place where students can easily be affected by sexual harassment. What a disgrace. How can we progress in our schoolwork if we are impacted and distracted by sexual harassment? We need to take action to inform others about this issue, to educate people on what sexual harassment is, and to take a step to end sexual harassment in school!

—Cyndi, youth organizer

givers—it thus became a key organizing point for GGE. My position also became full time.

When Sisters in Strength was started in January 2005, we had no idea it would grow into the program it is today: a paid, yearlong youth organizing internship for teen girls of color who advocate for the enforcement of sexual harassment policies in the New York City public schools through awareness-raising workshops and direct action.

When we were approached by the Educators for Children, Youth and Families to team up with a substance abuse prevention program called SPARK, housed in Paul Robeson High School, to offer empowerment workshops to the young women, we had never worked with high school students. The Educators for Children, Youth and Families wanted us to address young women's issues such as avoiding gangs and respecting their bodies by "acting like young ladies" (read: staying inside the box of oppressive, traditional, feminine gender roles). I was skeptical about how I could mesh what the school was asking for with GGE's mission of social change and philosophies of Freirean pedagogy that one must work *with* and not *for* the oppressed. They seemed to want me to reinforce the status quo, and I was interested in dismantling it. Taking a risk, I walked into the doors of the SPARK office with nothing more than a notepad, a pen, and one question for the teen women: What do you want from a weekly program that is just for girls?

Paul Robeson High School is located in Crown Heights, Brooklyn, a neighborhood where gang violence is so common that kids talk about people getting killed in one breath and what a hot mess Kanye West is in the next with no change in emotional affect. It's a topic of conversation like any other. The school's location and history of internal violence means that it is a scanning school: Every day when young people come to school they are subjected to metal detectors and searches of their bags and their persons before they are allowed to fully enter the building. Potential contraband (e.g., cell phones, iPods, cameras, etc.) is confiscated and the school feels like it is on lockdown from the moment you walk through the door. According to the New York Civil Liberties Union, there are fifty-two hundred police officers working in the New York City public schools, making the NYPD's School Safety Division the fifth largest police force in the entire country. This presence reinforces both the vulnerability of youth of color and fear of them, on a daily basis. It also increases the feeling that schools are not safe spaces for students and adults.

I had just given birth to my daughter, who is now three years old, and Sisters in Strength gave me the courage to let everyone know that I stand for something, that I'm not just some statistic. I learned that I am a smart and beautiful young woman who doesn't have to let having a child end my life. Life goes on and I am going on too. I am a fighter who will succeed and become a great member of society. I have a lot more confidence than I had before this experience.

—Jazmine, youth organizer

Sitting in the SPARK room, ten young women of color eyed the twenty-something white lady like she'd done lost her damn mind. This is not what Ms. Gooden, the SPARK program facilitator, had told them was going to happen in Sisters in Strength. Ms. Gooden had said they'd get free food and talk about things particular to being young ladies. The silence following my question was tangible—but then one of them spoke. And then another spoke. By the end of the hour, I had filled several sheets of paper with their ideas, and the girls and I had come up with a plan.

"I want to learn self-defense," said Keisha. She was a tall, tough girl with cornrows and a deep love of Alicia Keys. Her sister, Tricia, dissimilar in every way except that they were twins, sucked her teeth and responded, "Why you always gotta be fightin' all the time? We should have a dance. Robeson hasn't had a dance in forever. You know, one where we can dress up and get a DJ." Suddenly, the girls all started talking at once, a cacophony of what they'd wear and whose boyfriend could pay for a limo to drive them the eight blocks from his family's brownstone to the school. I thought I'd lost them for a minute until . . .

"So, if we have a dance, what will it be for exactly? I mean, how will people who come to the dance know it was organized by girls who care about women's empowerment?" I warily asked. Stumped silence. Eyes fell to the ground or climbed to the ceiling to avoid my gaze. I allowed the moment of reflection to linger, even when it became a little awkward . . . maybe a little painful. Then, "Because it'll be a benefit! Ooh, yeah. We can raise money for a cause, like a domestic violence shelter or something," said Cassandra, a short, light-skinned girl from Guyana whose sparkling eyes always held a smile. We had liftoff—a feminist combination of the twins' ideas of women's safety and fun.

The rest of that first meeting consisted of sketching out a weekly schedule of both educational workshops on topics the girls said they were interested in (HIV, self-defense, financial literacy, reproductive health, practical steps toward reaching future dreams, help with applying to college and for scholarships, healthy cooking lessons, and sexual privacy rights, to name a few) and a task timeline for coordinating the fundraiser. Each girl agreed to handle one area—poster design, publicity, getting a free DJ to spin—and all agreed to sell tickets. The tasks took place outside of the educational workshops, though a short time was reserved for a status check each week.

> When Sisters in Strength came to Paul Robeson High School, I was happy and excited. I told myself that I could be a good example for the younger girls in the group. When we decided to have a dance, I was so grateful but also scared at the same time. When we decided we were giving the money to help victims of domestic violence, I was even happier to do it. I couldn't wait to get started. It was a huge success and a lot of people supported our work. I still lead by example, like how to carry yourself as a young woman, and how to have respect for yourself and other people.
>
> —Trisha, youth organizer

Initially the girls tested the process by showing up late, not taking the content seriously, or sometimes not showing up at all. It was frustrating, but with the support of interns, we remained persistent with outreach and reminders. We also remained consistent by delivering the activities we promised them and always showing up on the days and at the time we had scheduled. The workshops helped to solidify group cohesiveness. With each disclosure, trust was established—and not just among the girls themselves. The girls also learned they could trust me—a white woman who was not from their community. This was enormously important because without that trust, the fire that was just building in this small group would have been extinguished when we hit our first challenge.

"The girls are looking for you," Ms. Roberts, the head security guard, informed me as I approached the sign-in desk one day. I raised my eyebrows and smiled at her. "What'd I do, Ms. Roberts? Am I in trouble?" She chuckled and shook her head. (Community Organizing Rule #2: make friends with people who hold true power. Principals may give you permission, but security guards, custodians, and secretaries give you information and access when it is most crucial.) "The principal said y'all can't be havin' y'alls dance in this school 'cause he doesn't want any problems in here. Ms. Gooden and the girls tried to tell him it's for a good cause, but he don't want to listen." I sighed and responded, "Well, working in schools ain't ever easy, is it?"

Flyer for fundraising dance to support Dwa Fanm.

Fortunately, the buzz of the dance had already spread among the students, and the girls weren't ready to give up without a fight. All we had to do was figure out what the concerns of the principal were and alter the plan to address those concerns. Over the next few weeks Sisters in Strength negotiated with the principal and vice principal, who finally agreed to let the dance take place only if (1) we could get at least ten adult chaperones from among the school staff, (2) the dance took place directly after school so no re-scanning had to take place, (3) no outsiders were allowed (read: no gang members who didn't already attend the school), and (4) the dance took place on May 27. The date was only two weeks away, but the girls were confident they could do what needed to be done. Now it was my turn to trust them—so I did.

The dance was an enormous success. Over four hundred students attended and it went off without incident. In two weeks the girls raised seven hundred dollars in ticket sales and donations, and the members of Sisters in Strength got their fifteen minutes of fame. The end-of-the-year celebration of their success took place in our meeting room with a buffet of curried chicken and rice, salad, and steamed vegetables. Farah Tanis, the founder of local domestic violence

Sisters in Strength participants award Farah Tanis (right) with funds raised from dance.

organization Dwa Fanm, attended the event to claim the donation and to personally thank the girls for their outstanding work raising funds for the organization's newly opened living space for women and children. It was during Farah's speech that it really hit the girls that what they'd done went beyond coordinating a school dance, and it was during that speech that we began to clearly see the potential for a group like Sisters in Strength in the work of GGE.

In late September 2005, a gym teacher was arrested for the ongoing rape and abuse of a female student at Paul Robeson High School. The rape began when the girl was fourteen years old, and continued for three years until she finally called the police at the urging of a friend. A week later the teacher committed suicide.

> I definitely thought I could trust Mandy and Janely (a bachelor of social work intern at GGE). If I, or any other girl in the group, had a personal issue, we felt comfortable talking to them about it, especially since there were times they both shared things with us about their own lives. They also made me feel like I could do anything I put my mind to, like when I felt I wouldn't be able to go to college.
>
> —Raquel, youth organizer

Students at the high school who spoke to the media refused to believe the allegations, even after the teacher took his own life. "I'm having a lot of doubts," said Alshika, sixteen. "He is a really good teacher; he never did anything or said anything weird." "I was surprised to hear it [that he had been arrested]. He was nice to everyone," Shukri, seventeen, said. "Personally I don't believe it. He never gave a bad impression to me or any of my friends."

This alarming news demonstrated the dire need for us to provide supportive programs for our girls. Joanne secured a second subcontract so that over the course

Leadership and Sisterhood Retreat, April 2006, Camp Chingachigook, Kattskill Bay, NY.

of the following year we were able to focus our efforts on working more closely with the girls at Paul Robeson High School. We wanted to know how they thought the program should shift in order to meet their needs and create a youth-led organizing model to work toward the mission of GGE. It was a challenge to keep them involved; the girls didn't readily embrace gender justice as their primary issue. Recruitment was always a struggle. Most meetings took place with five to ten girls in attendance because of competing responsibilities. Several girls from the first year were unable to continue because familial obligations took priority; they were expected to pick up and take care of younger siblings after school or seek part-time employment to contribute to their household income and save money for college. At the same time, GGE began getting phone calls from parents of teenage girls who didn't attend Paul Robeson High School asking how their daughters could get involved in Sisters in Strength. One young woman trekked across Brooklyn in order to attend the group.

The girls who remained, however, were deeply committed to the mission of Sisters in Strength. They wanted to get more hands-on experience with planning events and activities, as well as community service. Despite expressing a sense of powerlessness and disenfranchisement, the girls were committed to impacting their communities positively and bettering their own lives. It was up to GGE to find the resources to further develop the program. We got to work writing grant after grant and soliciting donations from community businesses and individual donors. By November 2006, GGE had raised enough funding to start the next incarnation of Sisters in Strength. GGE put out a call for high school girls from all over New York City to be part of our youth organizing program. Sisters in Strength grew beyond the walls of Paul Robeson High School that year, reborn as a community-organizing internship for all teen women of color, and moved into the GGE office.

The 2007–2008 cohort of Sisters in Strength signed on to organize around gender justice issues affecting their lives, and to be accountable as role models and mentors to middle school youth in GGE's newly developed after-school program, Urban Leaders Academy, which served boys and girls. The girls involved were representative of the diversity within their commu-

Cultures & Traditions
Perpetrate
Domestic Violence

Stop The V lence Now!!!

Urban Leaders Academy presentation, 2007.

nities, including pregnant and parenting teens; first- and second-generation immigrants; lesbian-, bisexual-, and queer-identified young women; and HIV-positive youth. The one thread of commonality among the teen women was a commitment to women's rights and social justice. This is the Sisters in Strength of today.

GGE met the girls' expressed needs by providing what was asked of the organization: an opportunity for skills building and paid work experience, a positive outlet through which one's abilities and talents could be constructively put to use, education on topics of interest, exposure to new ideas and perspectives, a safe environment to gain peer support, one-on-one counseling and mentoring from trusted adults, and most important, a space where one's personal growth was transferred into community-based actions to create positive change.

We are sisters who are strong young women of color following the example of those who came before us to raise awareness about the issues that affect us.

We strive to deconstruct stereotypes and stigmas that plague young women.

We are determined to create a safe space for girls to help and learn from one another.

We are fighting for equality and learning what it means to be a female activist.

We are advancing our skills as leaders to help others have a brighter future.

United, we create strong bonds for change and social justice.

We weave ourselves to form a quilt of compassion and fortitude.

Though we are young, we have a voice that deserves to be heard!

Sisters in Strength Mission Statement,
November 2009

The Street Harassment Summit
Mandy Van Deven

The newly formed Sisters in Strength chose street sexual harassment as their raison d'être because of the prevalence of public violence in girls' and women's daily lives. After the girls watched Maggie Hadleigh West's stunning documentary *War Zone*—which follows a woman as she walks alone in several major US cities and turns the camera on the men and boys who harass her by making sexual comments, gestures, or other overtures. West asks them why they believe their behavior is acceptable. The girls were inspired to make a film of their own. I, however, needed a little cajoling, not because I wasn't enthusiastic about the idea, but because I was concerned that GGE didn't have the capacity to bring this ambitious plan to fruition. We didn't have any prior experience with film, nor did we have resources to buy the necessary equipment to make a proper documentary. New Sisters in Strength member LaTosha, however, knew somebody from the Malcolm X Grassroots Movement who had film experience and could help.

Once LaTosha's friend was on board to provide technical assistance, the pieces began to fall into place. Since the Sisters in Strength documentary would be a short film (initially the girls envisioned it as a three-to-five-minute public service announcement, but it ended up being nearly twenty minutes long), a longer

Street Harassment Summit flyer.

film would need to accompany it in order to draw a significant audience for a screening. A screening alone didn't feel adequate without a discussion afterward about what had been seen, which would require that groups come out to talk through different aspects of street harassment. And since everybody knows that if you offer free food, people will come, food was the final element added to the event. What started as a seemingly unattainable idea, to make a public service announcement, turned into the Street Harassment Summit, a multifaceted event organized by Sisters in Strength, college interns, and staff.

Since there was mixed enthusiasm in the group regarding the technical aspects of making a film, those who were more excited about organizing the event itself took on the tasks of contacting groups with which to collaborate, soliciting food and prize donations, finding an adequate space to hold the screening, and publicizing the event. After numerous phone calls and dead ends, the girls found the perfect accommodation in Marta Valle Secondary School, whose Grand Street Settlement program agreed to co-host the event. Seven organizations agreed to facilitate workshops after the film—Girls Project/Boys Project,

> Getting behind the camera felt empowering and allowed us to take action just for ourselves, not even for anyone else. The fun was learning there is psychology behind every shot, that's why there is so much power in media; while holding the camera you can control what you shoot and zoom in on as it relates to the question.
>
> **—Ashley, youth organizer**

Ashley,
Hey . . . Shorty!
director.

Hollaback NYC, Audre Lorde Project, Mount Sinai Sexual Assault and Violence Intervention Program, Filipinas for Rights and Empowerment, Generation Q, and RightRides for Women's Safety—on topics including organizing a movement against sexual harassment in order to create a culture of respect in your school; improv acting to feel empowered, safe, and sexy in public spaces; understanding connections between anti-LGBTQ street harassment and harassment against women; and how to speak up when you're a bystander witnessing sexual harassment. In the meantime, Ashley took the reins and became the film's lead director.

Evelyn
Age 20

Hey . . . Shorty! documentary still.

Sisters in Strength's film *Hey . . . Shorty!*, the namesake of this book, premiered at the summit alongside *War Zone*. *Hey . . . Shorty!* blew everyone away with its candid exposure of the myths and realities of street sexual harassment experienced by young women of color; its hard-hitting examination of the root causes of why men feel it is their right to approach women they don't know, in ways both friendly and violent, in public spaces; and its identification of street harassment on a continuum of violence against women. Along with the attendees, the Street Harassment Summit was the first time the GGE staff saw *Hey . . . Shorty!* We had trusted Ashley when she said she had the film under control, and we felt like proud mamas when the credits rolled. The film, which went on to win the Best Youth Documentary Award at the tenth annual Roxbury Film Festival in Boston, offered something special: the unique and powerful perspective of teen girls of color. It also provided GGE with an organizing tool with which to begin conversations with youth and adults about street sexual harassment's impact on young women and men.

A man of color responds to being asked, Why do men aggressively harass women?

We holla at women. If they don't [respond], some people get violent, some people don't. I may tell them "Have a nice day," my man may tell them "Fuck you" and throw a bottle at 'em. Because women is out here looking for women . . . God said when women start liking women and men start liking men, the world is over. We're not looking for the world to be over. We're just trying to make it continue. It's gotta take a man and a woman to create the next child and make the world go round.
—From *Hey . . . Shorty!* documentary film

The response to *Hey . . . Shorty!* wasn't something I was prepared for. Looking at the room full of women who came to the summit—they were all so different—which showed me the magnitude of the problem. It was a wow factor. I was shocked and felt like taking a step back, realizing the magnitude of this problem.
—Ashley, youth organizer

Participating in the Street Harassment Summit with Sisters in Strength led me to declare a double major in black studies and sociology with a concentration in human services. I have yet to work with any other organization doing community organizing, but it has become a passion of mine and I will try to incorporate that into any of my future jobs/internships.
—Latosha, youth organizer

For the final part of our street harassment campaign, we created a poster to spread the message that New York State law prohibits street harassment within our community. The girls began the process by discussing what they wanted the poster to reflect, and then sketched out their ideas. They presented their concepts to Ari Moore, a local activist, artist, graphic designer, and illustrator. She translated their vision into this "Street Harassment is a Crime!" poster (see below).

Poster campaign led by Sisters in Strength. Designed by Ari Moore.

As the girls canvassed the neighborhood with the poster, they spoke with storeowners about how unsafe they felt in their community. They expressed why it was necessary for the stores to function as safe havens for women and girls who might be experiencing street harassment or who might need to enter to escape being followed. Many business owners agreed to offer a safe space for girls and women who were being harassed. As allies, they committed to prohibiting their employees from harassing girls and women, and prohibiting men from using their storefront to harass girls and women. Our multifaceted street harassment campaign brought media coverage from local papers and radio shows.

The Title IX Task Force
and the World Against
Sexual Harassment Campaign
Mandy Van Deven and
Joanne N. Smith

During the 2005–2006 school year, the term "sexual harassment" was removed from the NYCDOE Citywide Standards of Discipline and Intervention Measures, most often referred to as the Discipline Code or simply the "blue book," which is the manual dictating appropriate student behavior for all New York City public schools. Our Title IX Task Force hit a wall. The removal of the term meant that while the behaviors associated with sexual harassment were still not permitted, "sexual harassment" as such was no longer identified as inappropriate—or even existing—according to the NYCDOE. The legitimacy of GGE's work was significantly undermined by this linguistic erasure, as students, parents, and school personnel no longer had the NYCDOE Discipline Code to back up their complaints.

In response, parents and school staff came together under the guidance of GGE to create the World Against Sexual Harassment campaign, a multifaceted attempt to protect students against sexual harassment, empower teachers to act when they saw students engaging in sexually inappropriate behaviors, and to hold school administrators accountable for their lack of action in preventing and addressing sexual harassment when reported. For the World Against Sexual Harassment campaign, the task force drew up guidelines and reporting procedures that were taken directly from the NYCDOE's Chancellor's Regulations and could be implemented within the school by a staff member who would act as a sexual harassment advocate. GGE worked with four Brooklyn schools—PS 44, PS 56, Middle School (MS) 61, and Public School/Intermediate School (PS/IS) 308—providing free health and fitness programming. In each of these schools the task force recruited one teacher who agreed to act as the sexual harassment navigator in their school, a point person who would handle the reporting paperwork of all infractions within the school, counsel the students involved in the incidents, and speak with the students' caregivers.

The task force also created three separate informational booklets—for students, teachers, and parents— that clearly defined what sexual harassment was, gave information on how to speak to a student who had been harassed, as well as the student who had been accused of harassment, and informed the reader about what steps one should take to report sexual harassment in one's school. A two-hour training was created for school staff to inform them of the reporting guidelines and procedures, detail the types of behaviors that constituted infractions, and convey their rights and protections as NYCDOE employees to help them intervene in situations of sexual harassment. The task force was confident it had covered all the possible objections that a principal might have to implementing the World Against Sexual Harassment campaign in their school. We were using the preexisting NYCDOE policy, we were not creating any additional work for the school itself, and we were taking steps to make the school a safer learning environment. We sent the following letter to the school principals outlining our objectives:

A task force of parents from PS 44, PS 56, and PS/IS 308 in Bed-Stuy, working in collaboration with Girls for Gender Equity, has created a campaign to address student-to-student sexual harassment in school. The World Against Sexual Harassment campaign involves parents, students, and school officials (teachers, administrators, security officers, crossing guards, etc.) taking steps to make these schools a safer place for students to learn and socialize. These steps include:

1. Conspicuously posting the New York City Board of Education sexual harassment policy (Regulation of the Chancellor A-831) as required by the New York City Board of Education including the contact information of the school's Sexual Harassment Advocates and the Region 8 Title IX Coordinator at the entrance of the school as well as in each classroom.

2. Having full definitions and reporting procedures (Regulation of the Chancellor A-831) as well as a Sexual Harassment Complaint Form (Regulation of the Chancellor A-831 Attachment B) available to students, parents, and school staff in an accessible area in the main office.

3. Identifying teachers in the school who will act as Sexual Harassment Advocates who the students can go to if they have a question about, or would like to report, sexual harassment. The teachers will be identified by the WASH logo on their classroom door and will complete a thorough training with GGE on sexual harassment (See Section II: Reporting Procedure of the Regulation of the Chancellor A-831).

4. Investigating all complaints of sexual harassment as outlined in Section III: Investigation of the Regulation of the Chancellor A-831.

5. Distributing student and parent guidebooks about sexual harassment as well as Regulation of the Chancellor A-831 in the first month of school to all students and parents as required by the New York City Board of Education.

6. Designating 15 minutes of class time each month for sexual harassment to be addressed in each classroom. This will then be followed up with a discussion about sexual harassment between parents with their children at home.

7. Providing a copy of and training on the Regulation of the Chancellor A-831 to all teachers as required by the New York City Board of Education.

What possible objection could be raised?

"Absolutely not! My school will not be labeled the 'sexual harassment school,'" the principal at PS 44 said. "I can see you've put a lot of work into this, but if PS 44 puts this in place, and the other schools in our district don't, then our incident reports will go up and no one else's will. That will ruin this school's reputation, and I will not have it. PS 44 does not have a problem with sexual harassment, and when a student claims she has been sexually harassed, we deal with it on a case-by-case basis."

This response was a devastating blow. PS 44 was the same school where a teacher told me it was the girls' fault they were being harassed by the boys, and if they didn't want the boys to act like that then they should stop taunting them by acting so aggressively. The teacher wrote off sexual harassment as the girls being the products of bad parenting, and the boys "just acting like boys." And a month earlier, the vice principal had completely ignored Lorrie, a fifth grade girl who had tried to get help after a boy in her class humiliated her at recess by pulling her shirt above her head to fully expose her upper body to a group of male classmates. Two friends rescued Lorrie by shielding the girl with a sweater while she resituated her shirt. Crying and humiliated, Lorrie turned to her teacher to take action, but feeling that (as a man) her situation was too sensitive for him to address, he sent her to speak with the vice principal, a woman. When Lorrie entered the school's office, she told the vice principal what had happened. Instead of giving her the support she needed, the vice principal simply instructed Lorrie to return to her class and, despite the administrator's promise take action, no one ever spoke to Lorrie again about the incident. The boy failed to receive even a basic acknowledgement that his actions were inappropriate, much less a punishment for the pain he had inflicted on his classmate.

Lorrie had signed up for GGE's self-defense program after participating in the gender respect workshops. When she told me about the incident at our next self-defense session, I felt frustrated to hear yet another story about New York City public school staff failing to adequately respond to a situation that was clearly an infraction of NYCDOE policy. Lorrie felt powerless to do anything except try to avoid her classmate and his friends for the duration of the school year, another six months. I urged Lorrie to speak to her mother about the incident, which she did, and after learning about her daughter's mistreatment, Tracy joined the task force to ensure that this type of incident did not occur again. Tracy was grateful to have an empowering outlet for her frustrations and one that she could trust to teach her daughter how to stand up for her rights. But the principal's rejection of the World Against Sexual Harassment campaign sent the clear message that Tracy and Lorrie's concerns would not be addressed otherwise.

What the task force hadn't considered before the campaign is that the schools had a political and economic incentive to sweep incidents of sexual harassment under the rug. The scope of our work had to shift from the micro level of focusing on individual schools. In order for our organizing campaign against sexual harassment to be successful, we had to shift our focus to work directly with the NYCDOE.

In early 2007, Joanne reached out to Iris Morales of Union Square Awards who had ties with two allies at the NYCDOE. We met with them to discuss the miscalculations of the World Against Sexual Harassment campaign and feel out how GGE might move forward with our organizing work. We learned that the NYCDOE was aware of the sexual harassment and gender-biased education going on in the schools, but was unwilling to do anything about it. Iris's friends were impressed by GGE's work, but knowing our limited capacity, they asked, "There are fourteen hundred schools in New York City. How is GGE going to work with all of them?" While applauding our efforts to monitor Title IX in the four schools with whom we worked closely, they said they couldn't help us: in their estimation, the NYCDOE considered gang violence and poor standardized testing scores to be "more pressing issues." We reiterated the imperatives of having and implementing anti-sexual harassment policies, not only to protect the students, but also to protect the NYCDOE from liability when incidents occur. But they were powerless, and although they had good intentions, they too felt the repression of bureaucracy. The meeting made it clear that combating sexual harassment was not a priority for the NYCDOE.

Although Joanne and Mandy were disheartened coming out of the meeting, we had gained important insight that made our next step clear: we were going to expose this injustice and campaign to demand change. We needed New York City-specific research that would demonstrate the prevalence of sexual harassment in the public schools, reveal the failure of school adminis-trators to address gender-based violence, and illustrate the detrimental effects that sexual harassment could have on both students' academic performance and their feelings of safety in school. Singular anecdotal evidence, such as the stories of Lorrie and Tracy, would not be enough.

We knew localized research was needed in order to move forward with our work. The NYCDOE didn't understand that addressing sexual harassment in schools could have positive effects on many interre-lated issues affecting academic performance, such as queer bashing, safety, self-esteem, and teacher protec-tions. Whoever names something has power over it, and we believed that evidence in the form of quanti-tative and qualitative data, gained from a representa-tive cross section of the entire New York City school system, could have the power to change their minds. At the very least, it justified the need for the work done by GGE and several other community-based organizations throughout the city. With empirical evidence, GGE and others would be in a better position to advocate for our needs, and to move forward toward real change within the school system.

Participatory Action Research (PAR)
Joanne N. Smith and
Mandy Van Deven

In May 2007, Joanne attended a conference on youth, gender, and violence where Brett Stoudt, a PhD candidate at the Graduate Center of the City University of New York, shared research focused on examining privilege in education, particularly in regards to heteronormative masculinities, whiteness, and socioeconomic status. Brett considered this work a form of research known as participatory action research (PAR). He defined participatory action research as a philosophy and method of science committed to democratic inquiry and reform.* By this he meant that from start to finish, the systematic research was co-conducted with students and faculty. With his help they constructed the methods, did the interviews, and analyzed the data.

---

*PAR is a popular education method that allows community members to imagine, design, and conduct the research. PAR positions the participant-researcher as both a teacher, who is an expert in her or his own experience, and a student, who gains understanding from other's perspectives. It combines empirical data collection with reflection on how one's personal experiences are connected to larger societal issues, and brings the information back to the impacted community in order to create effective change on these critical issues. PAR challenges traditional methods of data collection, and is an especially powerful tool for communities of color, whose voices are often silenced or ignored.

We decided that participatory action research was just what GGE needed to prove to the NYCDOE that sexual harassment was a major problem that they couldn't ignore. Given what we had learned about the capabilities and enthusiasm of the teen women in Sisters in Strength while working on *Hey . . . Shorty!* and the Street Harassment Summit, we knew that they should be the ones to implement a participatory action research project on the state of sexual harassment in the New York City schools. After all, who was a better expert on the lives of teen women than teen women themselves? They were the ones being harassed, witnessing the harassment of others, and seeing the school staff's failure to act on the victims' behalf. They also knew what they needed in order to feel supported, respected, and safe.

Traditionally, research is gathered by professionals working within academic institutions who rarely include the voices of those directly affected by the conditions being studied, and the information gathered is usually not presented within the community for whom it would be most useful. We believed that in order to confront the multiple layers of discrimination that our communities faced, community members needed to be the ones to define issues, develop strategies for action, and act as their own advocates. The young women in Sisters in Strength didn't need an outside professional to come into their communities to tell them what was wrong or how to fix it when they were fully capable of making that assessment, coming up with recommendations for strategies to effect change, and implementing those strategies themselves. Through PAR, GGE sought to foster shared responsibility in improving the school environment for youth—especially young women and LGBTQ youth. Joanne contacted Brett, who introduced her to his colleague, Sarah Zeller-Berkman, a PhD candidate and researcher at the Public Science Project at the City University of New York's Graduate Center.

We had already opened up the Sisters in Strength program to all teen women of color attending public schools in Brooklyn, the Bronx, Queens, and Manhattan; we then made a concerted effort to reach far and wide to find the young women who would lead the PAR project. Mandy sent flyers out to every high school in the four boroughs and contacted every after-school program leader she could find to help her disseminate the Sisters in Strength application. The effort paid off: over two hundred girls applied. After an intensive application and interview process, Sisters in Strength was a group of ten teen girls who represented each of the four boroughs, various ethnicities and countries of origin (from Tibet to Bangladesh to Nigeria to New York City), different sexual orientations (bisexual, lesbian, and straight), and a range of skills to bring to the table. At the start of the 2007–2008 year, none of the girls in the youth organizing internship knew each other, but over the next year, they would laugh, argue, and feel frustrated with each other—in short, truly become like sisters.

Many of the teen girls had no prior experience uniting with others to speak out against injustice, and for this reason, it was important that the young women became familiar with the concepts behind social justice and the different strategies for organizing and advocacy on a grassroots level, before diving into the work. In addition to becoming familiar with the accomplishments of past Sisters in Strength groups through a screening and discussion of *Hey . . . Shorty!*, and visits from past Sisters in Strength members, the new cohort went on a New York City youth organizing tour to meet youth leaders at other local community-based organizations. At the New York Civil Liberties Union's Teen Health Initiative, Make the Road by Walking, and the Urban Youth Collaborative, the members of Sisters in Strength learned about the links between different social justice issues, witnessed how other youth organizers worked collaboratively, and started to understand the importance of GGE's work in the larger social justice movement. These meetings also helped the young women to better understand their own communities and build analytical and grassroots organizing skills as the next generation of movement leaders.

When I first became an intern and heard that we would be working on the topic of sexual harassment, I wasn't all for it. There were some things you didn't talk about much, and that was one of them. I was thinking that I didn't want to go around talking to people about this. I'm not saying I didn't believe sexual harassment was important, but you don't hear people talking about it often. After starting the project, I realized that it's a much bigger problem. It's not just that boy tries to touch you. It's you being afraid to go to school because of that boy. There are so many cases of sexual harassment. When you are afraid to live your own life because of it, something has to be done.
—Nadia, youth organizer

Once the teen women had a firm understanding of social justice, it was time for them to move to the next step of seeing *themselves* as agents of social change, and understand the context of GGE's mission to combat gender-based violence in the New York City public schools. The group had been told when applying for the position that they would be working on sexual harassment research, but they lacked the buy-in and understanding of the topic necessary to jump into forming a research study. And, as had happened in our gender respect workshops, the topic of sexual harassment raised a lot of conflicting emotions and opinions.

Although the girls didn't all agree on what sexual harassment was or how much it was a problem, all of them agreed they had experienced it. Most said they experienced it on a weekly or even daily basis. In order to get everyone on the same page, we brought in a list of questions about sexual harassment and asked the girls to research the answers independently and bring their results back to the group to be discussed. We didn't view it this way at the time, but in retrospect, the assignment was a sort of mini lesson on data collection in the form of a consciousness-raising session. Since we didn't know anything about how PAR worked, and were learning the theory and practice of the process from Sarah alongside the girls, we focused on deepening everyone's understanding of the issue.

Aside from the investigation into existing research, the young women reflected on experiences of sexual harassment and the feelings of anger and powerlessness it brought up for them. As sexual harassment became a more frequent topic of conversation at the meetings, the girls shared their own stories of being propositioned in the hallway and in classrooms, having other students touch their bodies without permission, and people spreading rumors about their sexuality or sexual experiences. Hearing other young women speak about times when they were made to feel uncomfortable and unsafe further opened the girls' eyes to the impact sexual harassment could have on their own emotional well-being, as well as that of those they cared about.

Schools should be, and are required by Title IX to be, safe environments for all students. It is painfully clear that schools are failing to ensure students' safety when they are "groped daily" or when their classmates declare it "grab-anything-you-want day," implying that they have a right to grab another person's body. One girl who participated in our research said, "A guy came up behind me while I was bending down, imitating sex acts." Another student told us that her "breast size [is] the topic of discussion on a daily basis." It is nearly impossible to learn or even go to school when you are forced to avoid peers because of your fear of "getting slapped/grabbed on the butt and breast" or someone screaming "suck my d***" at you.

Delving into their own experiences became an important ritual for the group. (Community Organizing Rule #3: self-care is just as important as social change.) In community organizing, the healing process is an integral piece of the work, and Sisters in Strength provided the time and space for the young women to heal from words and actions that had caused harm. When they joined their peers in GGE's cramped office space and made themselves a plate of food, they knew whatever they had to say—from complaints to jokes to social criticism—would be received with interest, enthusiasm, and thoughtful feedback.

Coming to terms with one's own experience allows a person to be a more effective changemaker. In realizing the similarities in each others' frequent and numerous experiences of sexual harassment in school throughout their lives, the conversations became more powerful. Sexual harassment wasn't something many of them had talked about before, and in sharing their stories, the personal became political. The girls saw the huge impact sexual harassment had on their education, self-esteem, and overall sense of safety as young women. This process transformed the issue from abstract to concrete. It helped build trust and intimacy among the girls, and gave a deeper meaning to the participatory action research work's eventual impact.

Training Youth Researchers
Sarah Zeller-Berkman, PhD

My first meeting with Joanne and Mandy about PAR took place in a tiny conference room in the GGE office. I was brought on board for my experience facilitating youth-led PAR projects throughout my doctoral work. Our conversation was mainly about logistics and time frame, but I was given a sense of the history of the project, and the impact that PAR would have on GGE's future community organizing. Joanne and Mandy believed that power in numbers would be necessary to provoke change from the NYCDOE. I agreed. Our goals were to make sure that the research maintained a sharp focus specifically on sexual harassment in schools, and that a survey would be a central part of the research design.

There can be challenges with meeting so many kinds of different people. Sometimes, the person is too quiet for your taste. Other times, they're too loud. Sometimes, when you're working on a group project, some people get lazy and don't want to do as much work as others and you end up falling behind. Other times, you have someone who wants to take charge and thinks they know better than everyone else. It's all about finding that balance and finding your voice so you don't end up just listening to everyone else.

—Nadia, youth organizer

It was apparent from the time I walked into my first meeting with Sisters in Strength that the young women sitting in the circle were remarkable. The motivation and power in the group was obvious as we began the icebreaker where everyone shared their names and what they felt they could bring to the research project.

At the start of a PAR project, it's important to articulate the strengths of those in the research collective, and to assess how those skills can be used to move the work forward. There was an impressive skill set in that small room.

We set out to get to know each other (a crucial starting point in all group work, as the interpersonal relationships within the group are integral to the collective research process that will require teamwork, trust, and many long hours of work). Given that research has generally been done "on" people, not "with" people, and that many young people are over-assessed in many areas of their lives, we openly discussed any negative associations with the word "research." I asked what came to mind when they thought of research and we had a brief discussion about their perceptions and fears.

We talked about the PAR process and defined PAR as "a methodological stance rooted in the belief that valid knowledge is produced only in collaboration and in action."* We discussed the fact that PAR recognizes those who are traditionally "studied" as experts of their own experiences, and how the PAR philosophy aligns with GGE and Sisters in Strength, who work for and within the community. The young women pointed out that they had joined Sisters in Strength because they wanted to address social injustice and create real change. Therefore, it made perfect sense to use a PAR design, which values the expertise of the community

*Institute for Participatory Action Research and Design.

being impacted by the injustice, to initiate change in the NYCDOE.

To give the young women a sense of what they would be doing, I spoke about some of the other youth PAR collectives with which I had collaborated. I shared a video that documented the PAR process undertaken by Children of Incarcerated Mothers, a group of young people researching, over the course of a year and a half, the stressors and supports for young people dealing with parental incarceration. I talked about their later work on a campaign in New York State with the Osborne Association to secure rights for youth with incarcerated parents. I passed around a powerful CD booklet about educational injustice that was created by another multiyear PAR project, Echoes of Brown. With these examples, the young women were beginning to understand the possibility and importance of the project they were about to embark on.

As we switched to the topic of sexual harassment, I went around the circle and asked each girl to share one experience of sexual harassment that she had either experienced personally or witnessed. Some girls shared their stories while a few made comments like, "Well, I never experienced sexual harassment, but I remember one time when I was telling the teacher that that number went on top, and he said, 'I bet you go on top.' Was that sexual harassment?" This conversation foreshadowed what would be the biggest finding in our research: sexual harassment in schools is completely normalized.

Although Mandy met with the group weekly, I came in only once every couple of months and advised

Mandy on how to proceed. By the time I visited the group a second time, the young women had done a lot of investigating into the topic of sexual harassment to get an idea of what others were saying about it and where there might be gaps in the research. They had come up with a series of possible questions for the project:

— Why do people sexually harass others?
— What is being done?
— What things are classified as sexual harassment?
— What are the borderlines?
— What triggers the harasser to participate in sexual harassment?
— How does society play a role?
— How do victims feel after they have been harassed?
— How does gender relate to sexual harassment?
— What is the typical age of sexual harassment victims?
— How did you feel when you were harassed?
— What was going through your mind?
— Did you ever seek help?
— Who did you blame for sexual harassment?
— What causes sexual harassment?
— Who does it affect?

To assess whether or not our questions would get to the root causes of sexual harassment, instead of just focusing on the individual level, we completed something called a "problem tree." Problem trees can be used in many ways, but in this project we used it to deepen the scope of our research questions. We explored some of the roots of sexual harassment, including sexism, the influence of mass media, and the prohibition of health classes under the Bush administration. At the end of the problem tree activity, we had our overarching research question: What is the impact of sexual harassment in New York City schools?

The next step was to design a research project with the necessary methods to answer our questions. This meant the young women would need to learn about the broad swath of methods available to them in creating their research design. Mandy coordinated a date when everyone could attend a weekend-long retreat for intensive training on research methods in the Poconos Mountains in Pennsylvania. Joanne made arrangements for lodging, transportation, and food (and a night of entertainment) that would facilitate a work environment that was comfortable yet productive.

After a long drive in a snowstorm, we arrived at the secluded rental house late on a Friday night with enough time to eat a group dinner and tell each other ghost stories before grabbing a few winks of sleep. Participatory research work embraces a strengths-based perspective, which acknowledges that the researchers have knowledge that is meaningful. One of the roles of the facilitator is to extract the existing knowledge in the group. So the next morning we began the actual training with a scavenger hunt. The young women worked in teams to find answers to questions like: How many people have a Myspace page? How many windows are in the house? Did anyone know what going on an international trip was like? These activities were designed to be fun approaches to observing, inquiring and/or quantifying phenomena. As we debriefed after the activity, we made the links between their success in gathering information for the scavenger hunt and the skill sets they would need to conduct interviews, make observations, and survey people.

We talked broadly about oppressed communities having some measure of control over the research produced about their experiences, and engaged in an intense conversation about the relationship between power and knowledge production. More specifically, we discussed the relationship between power and who controlled the media or who generally got to be labeled the "expert" on the institutions or experiences that impacted their lives.

Talking about why we were interested in doing this PAR project and how power and knowledge intersected brought us to a pointed conversation about standpoint theory. Standpoint theory asserts that one's position in society influences the way one views the world and assumes that all standpoints are partial and coexist with all parts of one's identity. We played a game where people picked an identity out of a hat (e.g., a gay man, a first-generation immigrant from the Middle East, or a really rich person), and answered a question from the perspective of the identity they had chosen. We asked questions like, "What do you think about supporting the war effort in Iraq?" The group realized the importance both of capturing different perspectives in our research design, and of acknowledging that the work we were creating was enriched by our own standpoints.

We then moved into the methods part of the training. The young women took notes and indicated which methods they wanted to know more about as I briefed them on fifteen different possibilities. We learned about journals and blogs, individual interviews, focus groups, collective and individual drawings, collage-making, slam books, surveys, participant observation, sentence completion, tailored walks/walk-throughs, and making cold calls.

After taking a very brief break for lunch we went more in-depth about the types of interviews and interview questions. After I modeled what *not* to do in an interview by putting on a brief skit, the young women broke up into teams to create their own protocol, to practice giving an interview, and to get feedback on their technique. We moved on to holding focus groups and discussed the types of information they elicit, such as group level data on perceptions, attitudes, or beliefs about a particular topic. I conducted a mock focus group in which participants were able to tap in and tap out of the role of facilitator, participant, and observer. After the young women were given the opportunity to practice running a focus group, we moved on to survey construction and implementation.

The girls studied examples of youth-created surveys, as well as surveys created by adults that have been widely used by young people. We talked briefly about some ideas for our own survey and how to use this methodology. The first day of training came to a close with a discussion about ethnographic data collection and participant observation. We read some examples of participant observations, and talked about note-

Clockwise from left: Chime, Tyleisha, and Sarah at PAR retreat, March 2008.

taking strategies, such as taking notes during or after an observation, and discussed what information might be important to collect. That night we made a hearty dinner of lasagna, salad, and garlic bread—comfort food after a long day of work. We then took the girls to a local bowling alley and video game arcade where they were able to decompress and enjoy the evening.

The next morning we reviewed anything that seemed a bit fuzzy from the day before, then had a discussion about the ethics of doing research. We collectively tried to problem-solve difficult ethical dilemmas that might come up in the course of their research. Thinking about the ethics of the research process was an important part of making sure our research team was both equipped for what could come up in the research process, and cognizant that even *asking* research questions has an impact on participants. The fact that the research process functions as a tool for action but also has effects of its own necessitates an awareness of both possibility and responsibility. Our group had a very sophisticated understanding of the ethical implications of the research process and products.

Just before wrapping up the training retreat midday, I asked the group to name one thing they were taking away from the retreat, one thing they would have changed about our time together, and which methods they were most interested in as we moved forward in creating the research project's design. Reflection is critical to PAR work as it deepens praxis and is key to developing critical thinking skills. We incorporated this necessary element throughout the research project.

When we returned to New York, it was time to design the research study and choose research participants. The Sisters in Strength interns decided to do a survey, focus groups, slam books (notebooks passed around in school, which contain written prompts for students to anonymously respond to), and a blog. Using different methods is useful in capturing a full picture of the phenomena of interest. They decided their goal would be to collect six hundred surveys from all five boroughs, including male and female students in both high schools and middle schools. We felt this sample size would garner statistically significant findings. The survey (on page 169) consisted of multiple-choice questions about how often sexual harassment occurred in school, who experienced it, and in what places students felt unsafe. We also asked youth about their personal experiences with sexual harassment, their responses to being sexually harassed, and the effects of harassment on their ability to focus in school. Finally, we examined students' awareness of the NYCDOE sexual harassment policy, and their opinions about whether school authority figures, such as teachers, security guards, and principals, and the NYCDOE, do enough to educate and protect students from sexual harassment.

Over the next three months of data collection, the young women in Sisters in Strength surpassed my wildest expectations about how many surveys could be collected. The youth researchers nearly doubled their initial goal, and ended up with 1,189 surveys of middle- and high-school students from over ninety schools in four of five boroughs (see page 117 for more details). Using grassroots organizing techniques, the researchers disseminated the survey to their peers during after-school programs, sent surveys home with peers, and

All of the teachers I asked to help me get the surveys distributed were incredibly helpful. They were very interested in what we were doing and were glad to distribute the surveys to their classes. My friends were willing to take the surveys since they are fun, but no one understood the importance of it. Sometimes people don't understand that there is a reason you make these surveys, and they make up bullshit answers. But for every person who gives a bullshit answer, there's someone who does care, who has been affected by sexual harassment and has a story to tell. So hopefully, with our surveys, our slam books, and our group interviews, we were able to show that it really is a big issue.

—Nadia, youth organizer

From left: Kyla, Nadia, and Christina practicing interviews, PAR retreat, March 2008.

held impromptu survey sessions at lunch and where ever they saw an opportunity. They recruited survey participants from all over New York City by reaching out to other youth-serving organizations. The girls spent hours inputting survey data and double-checking to insure that the information was being input correctly.

In addition to collecting surveys, the group conducted three focus groups with youth from local organizations. Each of these group interviews was facilitated by Sisters in Strength youth researchers who guided the group through a series of questions to elicit responses about experiences with sexual harassment in school. Using this methodology the young women were able to gain more extensive survey data and a deeper understanding of sexual harassment in schools. These conversations were really powerful in illustrating just how normalized sexual harassment had become. People didn't often recognize the profound impact it had until they were offered time to reflect on it.

In May 2008, the GGE staff and Sisters in Strength interns went on a PAR data analysis retreat in Lake Harmony, Pennsylvania. The goal of the retreat was to process the data from their survey and to come up with preliminary recommendations for future actions. I co-facilitated the retreat with Sabrica Barnett, another CUNY researcher, who trained the girls on statistical protocol for the social sciences, data analysis, and report writing. We applauded the girls' sample size, data input, and verification process, all three of which far exceeded the expectations of post-graduate level research.

This retreat was just as intense as the first one as we pored over reams of data outputs and charts representing various types of analysis that had been run to sort out the information. Since some of the survey questions were open-ended, we had to analyze them by reading and categorizing hundreds of responses. We worked in small groups for hours, and ultimately came up with our biggest finding: sexual harassment was rampant and, therefore, completely normalized. We ended the retreat actively thinking about ways to share the data. Some of the ideas generated were to create a know-your-rights card, perform skits that exemplified pieces from the data, and to draft a full report on the findings to send to the NYCDOE. Although there was a lot of energy within the group to disseminate the findings to multiple audiences, the magnitude of the project made the wisdom of working in coalition with others evident.

The Gender Equality Festival and the Coalition for Gender Equity in Schools (CGES)
Meghan Huppuch

It was raining on my first day as a college intern at GGE. My internship hours didn't officially start until the following week, but Mandy, my new supervisor, had asked me to come get acquainted with the Sisters in Strength interns at their weekly Friday evening meeting. Home for the holidays, I took a train and two subways to get from Ossining to Central Brooklyn, arriving around three p.m. for the four o'clock meeting.

A few weeks before, I had interviewed with Mandy Van Deven, then GGE's associate director. Her office, which was covered with social justice posters that said, "Question Gender" and "Feminism Spoken Here," immediately drew me in. Raised in a family of self-identified feminists, I felt like I was entering the space that I had been searching for: a place to explore and grow my passion for social justice. Five minutes into the interview with Mandy, I knew I wanted to spend at least the next four months at GGE.

"During your internship you'll work with Sisters in Strength on their research about sexual harassment in schools," Mandy said. I had no experience of any kind with research. I had never attended a New York City school, and at the time, I didn't even think I had much personal connection to sexual harassment. Despite my strong concern that I lacked expertise, in what I was soon to recognize as the GGE spirit, I jumped right in.

Several minutes past four on that rainy January day, we finally got settled in and the Sisters in Strength meeting began. Nine youth organizers, Mandy, and I were seated in a circle in the cramped conference room at GGE's office. I felt like an intruder—they had done this without me countless times before. I looked down at my ladybug rain boots and hoped they would give the young women a glimpse of who I was, maybe even help break the "this is my first meeting" tension. But as soon as introductions were out of the way, the two-hour period that followed foreshadowed my time working with Sisters in Strength. The girls had conversations about GGE work, school stresses, and what everyone thought of my boots—and all throughout, there was laughter. There had been no need for my nerves.

As I co-facilitated meetings throughout the remainder of the school year, we wondered aloud why we had never had conversations about sexual harassment in school before. The young women in the room attended different schools in various boroughs, and yet, everyone had the same experience when it came to sexual harassment—it was never talked about or addressed in school. How come none of us did anything about it before? Hadn't we seen it all the time? Did we just think it was normal? I say "we" because in working with Sisters in Strength, I connected with my own memories of sexual harassment in school. I recalled experiences I hadn't named before. It dawned on me that I had been silent about sexual harassment countless times. I had "enjoyed" the attention and felt that it validated me as a young woman; but I too had felt uncomfortable in my own school.

Memories of what I had considered "normal" flooded my mind: a friend bouncing a coin off my butt; sexual comments about my body in the hallway; a song about my sexual activity that was sung, loudly and repeatedly, in front of the entire cafeteria. I witnessed similar or worse things happen to my friends. This new awareness strengthened my passion as an activist more than I could have ever anticipated. As the months progressed, the conversations between the young women during meetings often included outrage over the frequency with which they saw sexual harassment happening so casually in their schools. And while the group's awareness and investment in addressing this pervasive issue grew, so did their desire to share this knowledge with other students in New York City schools.

We conducted PAR in order to amplify the voices of students. After data analysis and some difficult conversations, it seemed impossible that we could create the kind of change we wanted without the help of others. Community organizing is an effective tool in creating social change because the more individuals are united for a cause, the louder and more influential their collective voice becomes. We would use the PAR results to encourage others to join in coalition with us. Students, activists, organizations, educators, and parents (stakeholders with power) united together would further support the research results, and show the NYCDOE, policymakers, and politicians not only what *really* happens in schools, but also exactly what needed to change. Collectively, we could shift the culture of New York City schools.

By May, Mandy was leaving for two years abroad. I was sad to see my mentor leave. But she prepared me well, leaving behind clear instructions on how to organize the upcoming Gender Equality Festival, and identifying the organizations invited that would become our allies in the fight against sexual harassment in schools.

The Gender Equality Festival, our annual summer event, was the perfect venue to introduce our work to the community. For three years the festival had provided an outdoor space for folks in our neighborhood to connect with community resources, learn skills like self-defense, and support local performers. This year we could share the research results and gain an initial commitment from community members and organizations to be a part of the Coalition for Gender Equity in Schools (CGES)—a first step toward building a network that supported GGE's work to end sexual harassment. Although my internship was winding down, I was asked to stay at GGE as the festival coordinator for the summer of 2008.

At the retreat earlier in the spring, three brave Sisters in Strength interns, Kayla, Agnes, and Veronica, committed to creating a presentation for the Gender Equality Festival. Kayla and Veronica were two of the youngest members of Sisters in Strength at that time—and both were powerhouse leaders. Agnes, a seasoned Sister, was headed off to college in the fall, but had the time and the passion to help make the presentation happen. They put together a Know Your Rights pamphlet and a fast facts sheet about the data, but they knew it would take more than pamphlets and facts to grab and keep the attention of the crowd. Veronica, a powerful spoken-word artist, brought in a poem she had written about the impact of sexual harassment. The poem inspired Kayla, Agnes, and Veronica to create a group performance. Throughout late June and early July, they arrived in the afternoon and moved aside boxes and chairs in the cramped GGE office to make space for their rehearsal. Driven and inspired by the research and their Sisters who weren't able to attend the festival, they worked diligently to create an interpretive dance that expressed the raw emotion of the poem. Their final product had to be fierce and captivating to represent the collective's work at the festival. And it was a true collaboration. Veronica wrote the poem, and Kayla and Agnes choreographed it.

A few days before their debut at the festival, they asked GGE staff to be the audience for their rehearsal. I was blown away. Veronica's poem spoke to the research findings, her own experience, and the experiences of her friends. Agnes and Kayla's dance complemented it perfectly, capturing the emotions that can accompany sexual harassment—shame, silence, anger, and the conviction to take action. I felt sure upon seeing it that folks at the festival would be moved to get involved in GGE's anti-sexual harassment work immediately.

On the day of the festival, Kayla, Agnes, and Veronica spent the early part of the day at GGE's table, sharing the fast facts sheet and Know Your Rights pamphlet and telling community members about Sisters in Strength's research. Around noon, they took center stage.

You and I We Have Something in Common

Veronica Tirado

I,
I, spray paint the minds of young women and men,
with large positive words like
Strong, Colored, Intelligent, and Change
I spray and I,
I straighten lines that were once curved and curve
lines that were once straightened
Because to me it just seemed the right thing to do.

The right thing to do?

Yes, because somewhere, some place, at some time
people lost sight
They were blurred, hypnotized, confused, and
locked down and, you and I,
were on the same page, we saw worlds so vivid,
so clear
That no poison was so toxic enough to distort
our vision
Our vision has brought us here
Because we know what story needed to be
publicized and re-perceived.
Because a wise woman once said if you can't
change reality, change your perception of it.

Our world, doesn't need a beautiful woman to feel the pressure of a penis behind her, as she leans forward to retrieve books out her locker for her next class.
The way our minds react to the sight of a sour lemon, his actions will always replay in her mind.

Rewind

Reach forward
Touch textbook
Come boy
Hard boy
Grab stomach
Soft Thrust

Pause

Krystal can you give me the answer to problem four?

Ugh, what?

That's what I thought, I want to speak to you after class.

Pause

Oh my god, what the— (sighs)

Our world, doesn't need to hear words yelled out
before an eruption of action in the hallway like
faggot, or baty-boy or chi chi man.

Fast forward

Dean's office
Three o'clock
Phone call
Hi, is this Ms. Thomas, an incident has occurred
where your son—

Pause

Was outed
Harassed
Put down
Shut down
And now
Lives in a shelter because he can't take on strikes
and ear-splitting tones of his mother's resentment.
Tumbling dominoes can also speak for his
dropping out of school because with no support
and daily experiences of sexual harassment,

he gave up on hope and abuse,
he gave up on his education.

Our world doesn't need to see past sexual
harassment because we don't
want young men and women thinking that this is
okay
They shouldn't have to fear sexuality
Because of what happens in reality.

The assault of words and sexual activity is never
welcoming
And like an onion layered with walls so thick
That as each layer is removed
Broken down
We see who it happened to
What really happened.
And we ask why it happened.

Because you and I, we've just uncovered a carpet
with a lot of stories
A lot of unsettled thoughts
Unspoken words
And you and I, we got something in common.

We're Going To Make A Change.

The performance went off without a hitch. Despite their various worries—forgetting the words, taking a misstep during the dance, disinterest of audience members—they rocked the amphitheater at Von King Park. But we were disappointed with the number of people who actually got to see it. It was about ninety degrees and sunny that day, and there was no shade surrounding the stage area. While the reaction of the people who had seen it was phenomenal, the rush of coalition members I had predicted didn't materialize.

Developing the Coalition

The festival did help us build a strong network. In order to determine who was interested in joining our coalition, we designed a survey for the organizations with tables at the festival. Volunteers handed out the survey during the last hour of the event, and collected them as folks left. Twenty-three organizations expressed interest in being part of the CGES. With so many folks ready to join our mission, Joanne saw the need for someone to be dedicated to getting the coalition off the ground and asked me to stay on at GGE, this time as a community organizer. I was ecstatic to continue with the work that had engaged me in new ways of thinking and pushed me to further develop my sense of self. But before I took my next step as a community organizer by following up with the surveys, we had to bring the new group of Sisters in Strength youth organizers on board.

That August, ten Sisters in Strength interns began at GGE. Initially it was challenging for the new group to grasp everything that had transpired the previous year:

developing a research question, collecting surveys, leading focus groups, entering and analyzing the data. It was dense. Luckily we had three returning members who could pass their wisdom and experience on to the new young women. Another ally, a guru of participatory action research and youth participatory evaluation research, Kim Sabo Flores, led Sisters in Strength through activities to help the group take the data and turn it into solid analyses. That Saturday, spent poring over numbers and graphs, brought the work and mission into focus for the new group.

Kim began by posing a question to the group, "What's the difference between never, rarely, sometimes, and frequently?" The categories had appeared several times on the survey, but in order to determine the meaning of the responses, this new group had to make some difficult decisions about what those words signified. The reactions in the room were mixed, and a cacophony of voices followed. Ariel, a Brooklyn girl with a funky sense of style, who was new to the group, managed to get everyone's attention, "We have no way of knowing how each person defines those words. Rarely could mean once a month to me, and once a year to you." There were nods scattered around the room. Then Shantu, a veteran intern who demonstrated her dedication by traveling all the way from the Bronx, spoke up, "But we at least know that sexual harassment is occurring when someone is experiencing it 'sometimes,' and a response of 'frequently' means that that person is experiencing it the most often out of anyone surveyed." I was in a room full of opinionated researchers. Then Kayla, another returning intern, brought it to life by saying, "What if someone told you, 'I rarely get harassed by my principal.'" Everyone in the room froze. That didn't sound right. In fact, it sounded wrong. All of the sudden "rarely" didn't sound like "never"; it sounded a lot more like "sometimes." And the group was not going to stand for minimizing any student's experience with sexual harassment.

In that moment it was established that if Sisters in Strength grouped "rarely," "sometimes," and "frequently" together, they'd be making a statement, stating their values: any occurrence of sexual harassment is unacceptable.

Presenting the Research to the Coalition

On October 21, 2008, Sisters in Strength walked into a large, borrowed office space armed with chart paper covered in intricately hand-drawn graphs to face a packed room of over sixty of GGE's strongest allies. This group included Girls Inc. of NYC, Legal Momentum, Day One, Red Hook Initiative, Center for Anti-Violence Education, Girls Write Now, Sadie Nash Leadership Project, Feminist Press, Real Men Don't Holla, NYC Alliance Against Sexual Assault, Paul Robeson High School, Global Action Project, Movement in Motion, Younger Women's Task Force of NYC, Independent Commission on Public Education, Health and Education Alternatives for Teens Program (HEAT), and Asian and Pacific Islander Coalition on HIV/AIDS (APICHA). The goal was to present our findings and decide on a collective plan to move forward. After detailing the participatory action research process, Sisters in Strength shared the results and analyses on sexual harassment. Despite being overheated in a stuffy room, the folks who joined us that afternoon were ecstatic over the work Sisters in Strength had done. They were invested and experienced in fighting sexual harassment and other forms of gender-based violence, but this was the first time they had seen youth-led research that could support those efforts. Many of us in that room had faced people—in our personal and professional lives—who told us that gender-based violence wasn't a problem, or that we shouldn't take it so seriously. Now this newly formed coalition, armed with data, could finally move forward with our mission for change.

As always, the next step after the meeting was follow-up. I called and met with folks one-on-one to hear their reactions to the data, talk about how collaboration would further our shared goals, and ask them to join us again the following month. Another large group was in attendance for the December meeting, where we began to shape our mission and values as a group.

One educator present didn't like the idea that we were discussing making New York City schools "safe": "I work in a school and I know that we're doing our best to create a safe environment for our students. It's not perfect, but we're working hard and most times we succeed." Everyone present heard her concerns and agreed to change the word to "safer."

Sarah Zeller-Berkman led us through the theory of change process and we agreed on the following: the purpose of the Coalition for Gender Equity in Schools (CGES) is to make New York City schools safer for all

students and free of sexual harassment using an inter-
sectional analysis of its causes. The ideas were flowing,
and the activists, organizers, educators, and youth in
the room created a list of what "safer" means: violence-
free; bully-free; harassment-free; no tolerance for
harassment/bullying—no matter students' identities;
conducive to learning; emotional safe space; less police
presence; freedom of self expression—wear what you
want and walk where you want; addressing violence
head on; respect for students' identities; competent
staff; and partnerships between youth, parents, teachers, and community members.

When asked, "How can we achieve safer schools?"
the first thing I heard from the group was "prevention." Another coalition member elaborated, "And in
order to prevent sexual harassment, education is vital.
If folks don't know what harassment is, how are they
supposed to stop doing it? Or speak up about it?"
Feeling impassioned, someone else added, "But what
we really need is a human rights framework in education! We need to create a bill of rights for students. It's
absolutely unacceptable that these things are happening in our schools—let's advocate for a *policy* to prevent it!" I stepped in, "While I completely agree, keep
in mind that Title IX has been in effect since 1972. If
it were implemented consistently, we wouldn't be fac-
ing this issue in our schools. We have the advantage of
being able to work within the existing framework and
challenge NYCDOE to utilize it more effectively." The
group agreed to investigate the existing policies: Title
IX, the New York City Discipline Code, and the Chancellor's Regulations.

Connecting with Students on the Issue

By January 2009, word about our work had spread throughout the city and created a demand for a workshop that would present our findings on sexual harassment. That same month, two women from the True Body Project would visit GGE and powerfully influence the way in which the SIS interns would move forward with the development of their workshop.

The True Body Project's mission is to empower girls to identify and connect to their true bodies, to grow authentic voices, and to advocate for the health and safety of girls and women everywhere. Led by two women, Sisters in Strength sat in a circle on the floor, and answered prompt questions: "I hunger for . . . ," "The language my body speaks is . . . ," "A good girl . . . ," "A bad girl . . . ," "My body has a secret and it is hiding in my . . . ," "My mother's body . . . ," "You cannot measure my . . . ," etc. The power and honesty of this exercise inspired Sisters in Strength interns to apply the same method of self-exploration to reach youth in their peer workshops.

Immediately after this experience, the Sisters in Strength interns began transforming the workshop they were designing. Not only would they screen *Hey . . . Shorty!*, lead a discussion, and provide information about student rights in schools, they would develop question prompts to discover how young women's self-esteem was affected by sexual harassment: "People see my body as . . . ," "I feel powerless when . . . ," "I regain strength . . . ," and "My . . . keeps me safe."

Furthering this theme, my fellow community organizer, Vanessa Nisperos, reached out to artists Carmen

Leah Ascencio and Chelsea Gregory who led Theater of the Oppressed workshops. Created by Brazilian Augusto Boal during the 1950s and 1960s, the Theater of the Oppressed workshops are used as an effective, creative, and empowering tool for educational and social change work by analyzing systems of oppression and power, and exploring group solutions to those problems.

The Saturday workshops explored personal experience, monologue-writing techniques, and Forum Theater training (a part of Theater of the Oppressed where an audience member can stop the performance to suggest a different action that could end the oppression being performed). From these workshops, a performance exercise titled "More Than Just a Touch" was created. Using her personal experience of sexual harassment, Chiamaka, a Sister in Strength intern, bravely chose to portray herself in this exercise. In the

Sisters in Strength 2008–2009 cohort.

story, she was in class and went up to hand in a paper. A young man made several sexual comments about her body loud enough for the whole class and the teacher to hear. When Chiamaka stood up for herself, the situation escalated, and instead of supporting her, the teacher demanded that both she and the young man leave class. In the exercise, Chiamaka played out her experience in front of an audience. The "spectactors" (Theater of the Oppressed workshops commonly use a combination of spectators and actors) then had the chance to yell, "Stop!" from the audience. At that point, that spectactor had the responsibility to come up and replace the protagonist, and act out what they believed would change the outcome of the scene. This was often more challenging than they anticipated when they submitted to the urge to yell, "Stop!" Whether they tried to persuade the teacher, or confront the antagonist directly, their actions often did not improve the situation. Eventually, a spectactor would come up and do the right combination of things to end the moment of oppression. This exercise allowed everyone involved to feel the difficulty and frustration one confronts in trying to change a situation.

It is hard to envision a school without sexual harassment. However, if one existed, I imagine it would be a place where kids can excel as students instead of having to worry about what is going to be said or done to them the next time they go in the hallway.

—Kai, youth organizer

Before this exercise was led in a workshop, it was announced that the scene was taken from a real life experience. Occasionally, a participant would insist that a teacher "wouldn't react that way." Chiamaka would then share with the group that this was in fact her experience. She spoke frankly about how real the portrayal was. Needless to say, each performance was moving and had a profound impact on the audience. I still encounter people who witnessed these workshops and comment on the intensity of this particular performance.

By participating in the Theater of the Oppressed workshops and monologue-writing work, the young women of Sisters in Strength challenged themselves by stepping out of their comfort zones and into a place where their experiences could be used to educate others. They couldn't have done it without amazing sisterly support from one another.

Reflecting on this scene in my life, and actually performing it with the rest of the Sisters in Strength, was instrumental in allowing me to see where the real problem lies in sexual harassment. Women and girls are often devalued, degraded, and demoralized by acts of sexual harassment, which is so embedded in our society that neither men nor women can identify it. Phil made me feel disgusted with myself. He made me second-guess what I wore that day, how my hair looked, and just me as a woman. His "compliments" were insults knowing the disrespectful connotations behind them. His looks were knives through my self-esteem.

Little did I know that Philip was also a victim, a victim of society's definition of what a man should stand for and how much power he should have. The same views have caused men throughout history to hold more power than women economically and socially. Much has changed but not enough for men and women to be called equals. This is where Girls for Gender Equity comes in. To educate boys and men like Phil, and to empower women and girls like myself. Taking it one step at a time, our goal is to end sexual harassment.

—Chiamaka, youth organizer

The NYCDOE Hearing

In the meantime, I was making failed attempts at reaching people in the NYSDOE and NYCDOE. Joanne suggested I contact Michael Moon at the NYSDOE who had acted as an ally to GGE. In the past, Michael had provided us with Title IX resources, a list of federal antidiscrimination laws related to schools, and answers to our questions about implementation. Even his most recent department's title—Professional Development, Race and Gender Equity—was a beacon of hope.

So I called him, but when I asked for Michael Moon, I was told that he no longer worked at the NYSDOE. Thinking that I'd just speak to whoever was the new specialist on Title IX I said, "Who can I speak to about Title IX?" The person on the other end of the phone paused, then said, "What is Title IX?" I was taken aback, but remained calm, "Title IX addresses gender equity in schools. I'm interested in speaking with the person who has taken over Mr. Moon's position in the Race and Gender Equity Department." Another pause. "I'm sorry but no one is doing that work anymore." In complete disbelief, I thanked the person on the other end and hung up. I hadn't anticipated hitting such a definitive dead end. This was not the first, or last, time that we met with resistance or disinterest when seeking information about sexual harassment. Luckily Vanessa had gathered reliable information from the NYC Alliance Against Sexual Assault that there was someone within the Department of Education who could be an ally to us. Eric Pliner turned out to be that and more.

Sisters in Strength at the NYCDOE hearing.

When we first met with Eric, Vanessa and I were unsure what to expect. But Eric proved to be a supportive contact: he offered us time, collaboration, and most importantly, information. It was through our relationship with him that we found out about the NYCDOE's Discipline Code Hearing in June 2009.

The Discipline Code was one of the documents that the coalition had looked into earlier in the year. While it doesn't dictate the rules, like the Chancellor's Regulations, it is the guide for how discipline is to be carried out in New York City public schools. It also outlines the New York City Students Bill of Rights and suggests Guidance Interventions, which can be used in place of, or along with, disciplinary measures in certain situations.

In preparation for the hearing, GGE held a focus group with youth and adults from the coalition. The questions to be answered at the meeting: What do we feel strongly that the NYCDOE should change about the Discipline Code? How can they make the way it deals with sexual harassment more effective? As we read through the Discipline Code, and examined the few sections about sexual harassment, many of the youth spoke up about completely changing the format to make it more youth-friendly and effective. In its current form, the structure of the Discipline Code makes it especially difficult to read, understand, and reference. Another suggestion was to take the infractions addressing sexual harassment and spread them out so that, instead of students getting suspended immediately, there would be lesser degrees that would require education in place of discipline. These ideas were incorporated into the written testimony.

On the evening of the hearing, thirteen members of CGES entered the Tweed building, NYCDOE's headquarters. An opulent old courthouse, the CGES youth wondered aloud, "Why does their building look like this, but my school looks like . . . that?!" A good question indeed; the marble columns and sea of plush office chairs made it look as if there were no deficit of funds for education in New York City. And yet, some New York City schools don't even have textbooks.

The Testimonies

Hello, my name is Brittany. I am an intern at Girls for Gender Equity and a member of the Coalition for Gender Equity in Schools. Thank you for this opportunity to speak about the importance of preventing sexual harassment and training school faculty and staff to recognize sexual harassment and take it seriously.

As a former New York City school student and an advocate for women's rights, I have heard and witnessed countless stories of sexual harassment. One thing that has stood out to me is how many times I've heard girls complaining of their school's "boys will be boys" attitude. This attitude excuses boys for certain behaviors that are expected of them—such as teasing, pranks, and sexual harassment. These same behaviors often target girls and lesbian, gay, bisexual, and transgender students. Because they are not prevented or dealt with effectively, they make schools unsafe and uncomfortable.

The administration, social workers, and teachers who are expected to deal with problems between students don't address the sexual teasing, touching, suggestive looks, and pressure for sexual activity that take place every day. These behaviors take place in our schools' hallways, staircases, classrooms, and lunchrooms.

Nefertiti testifying during the hearing, 2008.

Sadly, many times when those who are being harassed are courageous enough to speak to authority about it, they are not taken seriously. Failing to address these behaviors sends students clear messages. One, they should expect to be sexually harassed and put up with it willingly. Two, student safety is not a priority. And third, speaking up for themselves will not make a difference. We are here today because we know our rights and these young people will not be silenced any longer. While necessary changes in the Discipline Code will encourage preventative measures, these changes in language do not guarantee that real change will be put into action. In order for our schools to truly become safer, the Department of Education must require that all school employees be trained in how to identify and intervene in sexual harassment, and also how to receive complaints of harassment. This is simply another step toward creating positive, safe, and equal learning environments.

Hello, my name is Nefertiti. I am a former New York City public school student. I am a Sisters in Strength intern with Girls for Gender Equity. I am also a member of the Coalition for Gender Equity in Schools. As a part of the coalition, Sisters in Strength has conducted research, designed workshops, and created a theater piece, all to educate and raise awareness about how hurtful it is for students to be expected to learn and grow in schools where they feel unsafe and threatened.

My peers and I are affected by sexual harassment every day, both inside and outside of school. We believe that any occurrence of sexual harassment is unacceptable. In the struggle to end sexual harassment, I believe it's important to debunk common misconceptions. Many people believe that boys don't get sexually harassed. The nearly five hundred boys that we surveyed reported most frequently experiencing sexual harassment in locker rooms, libraries, after-school hours, and at security stations.

Others believe that the harassment of individuals who are lesbian, gay, bisexual, and transgender is not sexual harassment. We disagree. Harassment about sexual orientation, gender identity, and gender expression are all forms of sexual harassment. We must unite with our LGBTQ friends and classmates and stop sexual harassment together.

Many more believe that words are not forms of sexual harassment. However, even verbal abuse poses the threat of violence, whether it is inflicted by the harasser onto the victim, or the victim upon themselves, as in the cases of countless young people across the country who have ended their lives just this past year in desperate responses to antigay harassment.

I also believe it's necessary to address the lack of support from administration in situations of sexual harassment. It is truly important to acknowledge that the problem does not lie within the individual being harassed, the problem lies within the external forces that perpetuate and enable sexual harassment to exist in a place like school, where all are supposed to feel safe. As policy makers who can create change in the Discipline Code and beyond, please take bold steps to create safer schools for all students. Make it clear which infractions include consensual behavior and which include nonconsensual behavior. Define clearly that the perpetrator, and not the victim of the actions, will be punished. Differentiate violent sexual harassment from nonviolent sexual harassment so that schools can prevent behavior from escalating and becoming extreme. Make conscientious decisions about language and what responses are matched to certain behaviors.

And lastly, include youth voices in the creation of the Discipline Code every step of the way. It's a set of rights and rules about us and for us. It would be an effective and powerful collaboration and we should have a say. Thank you for providing this venue for us to speak today.

When I testified on behalf of Cammie, a young woman who was not able to be there, I asked the folks who were supporting CGES to stand where they were to demonstrate our strength in numbers. With no more than thirty people in attendance overall, our group of thirteen was impressive. The NYCDOE officials who oversaw the hearing expressed interest in our ideas for a table of contents and glossary of the Discipline Code, but apparently the rest of what we said didn't strike them as important. While we have continued to build a relationship with NYCDOE, they have yet to adopt our recommendations.

Gym Class Criminal

I don't wear skirts or dress really feminine for school. I usually wear girl's t-shirts, skinny jeans, and rain boots because my identity almost seems like a threat to everyone. Me being me means that I am different and deserve to be slaughtered in every way possible. Some people confuse the term hermaphrodite or transsexual with the fact that I do not conform to this made-up gender construct. Transgender or gender nonconforming simply means that I dress and act as I feel. But not too many people understand how simple it is.

"For you to be a boy, you shouldn't look like this. You look real feminine."

That's what he told me as he stroked every reserved element of my body. It wasn't for him. My beautiful brown skin was not set aside for him! I am not anyone's sex toy, sexual experimentation, or grounds for a sexual explosion. He continued and all I could hear was a strong, bottomless tone, but I couldn't hear him. I couldn't hear his words. It was as if my eyes were frozen by a global blizzard and I could feel my legs tremble as my body disconnected from my intellect. I just knew he was attacking me and I could do nothing about it. That's when a teacher walked in and he released me. They both acted as if nothing had happened. Walked out the doors and moved on with their lives. Even though mine had stopped.

It happened last year in the locker room, at the end of gym class. I was in my wifebeater and underwear, getting my clothes from the locker when he rushed up on me. He propelled my body up against the rusted lockers and it felt like I could only endure being pinned between the lockers and his basketball-built body. My body had no sense of authority, whereas his explored the phenomenon of masculinity and being a man.

I felt so puny, like I should've done more. My back was completely sore and my arms bruised from his forceful grip. When I would see him in the hallway he would lick his lips and smile. It was disgusting, degrading, and so disturbing. On most days I would go home to take showers to attempt to release his presence that lived within the pores of my skin. I tried to scrub away all the thoughts that lingered. I tried but the stain still remained. My skin would turn to flesh, and rivers on my cheeks were the only means of calming my nerves.

Ultimately I knew I had to tell him how I felt, while no one was around. I didn't want him to do it to anyone else. I didn't want anyone else to have to be afraid or feel paralyzed by his touch.

Handsome, no. You are repulsive, less than a man, less than the dirt that I walk on. If I had the muscle I would have shattered your earth, your soul and fortitude, just like you did mine! What you did to me last year made me feel terrified of you. But I'm not mad at you because you gave me an experience. Your hands and words are going to allow me to strive harder for what I want. It doesn't make you any bigger than me. In actuality, you're smaller than me. And think about it, if you continue to do this to people you're not going to be happy at all. You can't hurt people because you're intimidated or for your own pleasure, you're hurting yourself inside.

—Written by Veronica Tirado, based on her interview with a young trans woman who talked about her experience with harassment in school.

Summary of the Research Results

Methodology

From September 2007 through May 2008, a team of nine Sisters in Strength researchers designed and implemented a participatory action research project to answer the question, "What is the impact of sexual harassment in New York City schools?" GGE and Sisters in Strength youth researchers began by defining the goals of the project based on extensive discussions among ourselves and with the community. The Sisters in Strength youth researchers developed questions collaboratively and decided upon four methods to obtain answers to them: a survey, focus groups, a slam book, and a blog. They used these research tools to collect quantitative data of students' experiences, which would provide the NYCDOE with proof that sexual harassment is a problem worthy of being addressed.

Our research represents the experiences of 1,189 middle school and high school (grades six through twelve) students attending over ninety different schools throughout Brooklyn, Queens, the Bronx, and Manhattan. We reached out to youth-serving organizations, partnered with teachers at our schools to distribute the surveys, and gave them to youth at other internships and jobs we held during our research. Sixty-three percent of respondents identified as female and 37 percent male. The survey participants ranged in age from eleven to twenty years, although the majority of students were between fifteen and seventeen years old. Our participants came from various racial and ethnic backgrounds, although most were youth of color, representing the diversity of New York City: 43 percent of participants self-described as Black/African American, 21 percent as Hispanic/Latino, 21 percent as Asian/Pacific Islander, 7 percent as White/Caucasian, and 8 percent as Mixed.

The survey (see page 169) consisted of multiple choice questions about how often sexual harassment occurred in school, at whom it was directed, and locations where students felt unsafe. We also asked youth about their personal experiences with sexual harassment, their responses to being sexually harassed, and its effects on their ability to focus in school. Finally, we examined students' awareness of the NYCDOE's sexual harassment policy and their opinions about whether school authority figures, such as teachers, security guards, and principals, as well as the NYCDOE, do enough to educate and protect students from sexual harassment.

We conducted three focus groups with forty youth from local organizations: Red Hook Initiative (Brooklyn, NY), Young Women of Color HIV/AIDS Coalition (New York, NY), and Lower East Side Girls' Club (New York, NY). Focus groups are a form of interviews that utilize collective communication between research participants, allowing for a deeper exploration of the topic than simply filling out a survey. Three to four SIS youth researchers facilitated each group and guided participants through a series of questions to elicit youths' experiences with sexual harassment in school. Youth facilitators prompted discussion by asking broad questions, such as "What is the definition of sexual harassment?" and "Who are targets of sexual harassment in school?" and then let group members have a discussion. When needed, youth researchers would ask group members to elaborate on a point.

A slam book is a notebook that is passed around between students in junior and high school. It contains written prompts to which students can anonymously respond. GGE and Sisters in Strength youth researchers' prompts included unfinished statements such as "Incidents of sexual harassment in school occur because . . . " and "The experience of sexual harassment in school that I remember the most is . . . " The responses to these prompts provided us with qualitative data about students' thoughts and opinions regarding the occurrence of sexual harassment in school. Due to the anonymous nature of the slam book, we could not calculate the number of people who participated, nor do we know their demographics. However, the slam books were useful for collecting several pages of data for each question posed below:

— Sexual harassment is . . .
— If I were blamed for sexual harassment in school I would be . . .
— The experience of sexual harassment in school that I remember the most is . . .
— The best way to deal with sexual harassment in school is . . .
— Gay/lesbian/bisexual/transgender students are targets of sexual harassment in school because . . .

— People who sexually harass others in school should be . . .
— When I spoke to someone after being sexually harassed at school . . .
— Incidents of sexual harassment in school occur because . . .
— The media influences sexual harassment in schools by . . .
— The blame for sexual harassment in schools should be placed on . . .
— Students sexually harass other students because . . .

New York City Public Schools Findings

We analyzed both the quantitative and qualitative data to find out the impact of sexual harassment in New York City public middle and high schools. Our research yielded three major findings that each incorporate subthemes: (1) in-school sexual harassment occurs in many ways, to many people, and in many locations, (2) sexual harassment is a "normal" part of young people's school experience, and (3) students want and need more education about sexual harassment.

Finding #1: in-school sexual harassment occurs in many ways, to many people, and in many locations.

When we asked youth whether they believed sexual harassment was a problem in their schools, most (69 percent) said they did not, with only slight variation along gender lines: 74 percent of males compared to 67 percent of females reported that sexual harassment was not a problem in their school. Seventy-eight percent of students (73 percent of females and 84 percent of males) said they had never been sexually harassed at school. However, when we asked students to tell us how often students in their school were sexually harassed, nearly a quarter (23 percent) said daily, 14 percent said weekly, 7 percent said monthly, and 23 percent said a few times a year. When students were given the opportunity to indicate whether particular behaviors that constituted sexual harassment occurred in their schools, participants indicated that every type of behavior listed in the survey occurred.

For an environment where most say sexual harassment is not a problem, there is considerable inappropriate sexual behavior going on in schools. Out of the students surveyed, 71 percent reported hearing sexual teasing, jokes, or remarks at their schools. Touching, pinching, or brushing against someone sexually and on purpose was reported by 63 percent of students and 60 percent had seen sexually suggestive looks, gestures, or body language. This is followed by whistles, calls, hoots, or yells of a sexual nature (46 percent); leaning over or cornering a person (39 percent); letters, phone calls, or Internet communication (34 percent); pressure for sex or sexual activity (31 percent); sexually explicit pictures or music on an electronic device (23 percent); pressure for dates (18 percent); and forced sexual activity (10 percent). Further analysis by gender showed that girls were slightly more likely than boys to report that "sexual teasing, jokes, or remarks" and "sexually suggestive looks, gestures, or body language" occurred in their schools. There were barely any gender differences regarding the other types of sexual harassing behaviors.

So where does harassment happen? Both males and females reported that sexual harassment occurred most often in staircases (57 percent), hallways (58 percent), and outside on school property (56 percent). However, girls reported high frequencies of sexual harassment in all of the aforementioned locations, as well as in the cafeteria/lunchroom (53 percent). Safer spaces with a low frequency rate included the security station (8 percent) and the library (12 percent); the majority of students reported that sexual harassment "rarely" or "never" occurred in these places. Despite the finding that the locker room had a relatively low frequency rate (30 percent), we did find that boys (34 percent) were more likely than girls (27 percent) to say that sexual harassment occurred there. This indicates that male students have knowledge of higher frequencies of sexual harassment in areas that are less populated by

I can barely breathe. I stop to catch my breath. Just take a pause, a beat, a rest. I cannot believe I am going through it because of a word I heard. As I walk through the halls, someone calls me by "name." Someone calls me by my shame. Curls their mouth to call me out. Twists up their lips in a distinct and distant shout of the word (I can barely say the word) "FAGGOT!" Before I even knew what gay was, somebody managed to find something to say about my limp wrists and effeminate lisp. So long as I am in this skin and my feelings toward men are still a sin, they will forever have it in for me as long as that word still exists to oppress me at my best and suppress my self-expression. Denied the support of teachers and faculty who tell me, sell me, some lines about how sticks and stones may break my bones but words can never hurt me. Words have always hurt me.

—Nefertiti, youth organizer

students of both genders, and where same-sex sexual harassment can be assumed to occur.

We asked youth who they believed to be the targets of sexual harassment, as well as the perpetrators of the harassment. Youth indicated that female students (81 percent), male students (71 percent), and LGBTQ students (64 percent) were all targets of sexual harassment.* The responses to this question showed that sexual harassment happened to students regardless of gender identity, gender expression, and sexual orientation. Participants also told us that students were primarily responsible for harassing other students, and 57 percent blamed other students the most for sexual harassment happening in schools. Fifty-eight percent of respondents reported that male students harassed other students frequently or sometimes, and 44 percent said female students harassed others. We believe this is because on a day-to-day basis, students have the most direct contact with one another in school. The groups with the next highest reported rates of sexual harassment were the groups that students had the next most contact with: security guards (10 percent), gym teachers (19 percent), and classroom teachers (7 percent). A

---

* The categories of female, male, and LGBTQ students overlap, and students who identify as LGBTQ may also identify as male or female. We believe bias-based harassment experienced by LGBTQ students is included in the category of sexual harassment because it is based on sexual orientation, gender identity, and gender expression. However, it seems the students did not define the harassment of LGBTQ students in the same way. This difference most likely affected the results of this question in that fewer students claimed that LGBTQ students were sexually harassed in school than claimed male and female students were sexually harassed.

small percentage of youth (3 percent) reported that the principal or vice principal sexually harassed students as well.

The research shows that sexual harassment takes place at all levels in the New York City public schools. Everyone from the students to the principals are engaging in harassing behaviors that are, for the most part, unaddressed. Because of its pervasiveness, two-thirds of students in New York City public schools consider sexual harassment to be a typical part of their school experience. While students initially asserted that sexual harassment was not a problem in their schools, the subsequent responses contradicted their previous statements. As the survey progressed, students seemed to expand their definition of sexual harassment, which revealed the reality of what was happening in their schools. Sexual harassment is a normalized behavior within the school environment, therefore while students see it happening, they do not believe that it is a problem, and they do not report it.

Finding #2: sexual harassment is a "normal" part of young people's school experience.

Despite students' assertions that sexual harassment occurs often, students do not report sexual harassment when it occurs nor do they consider sexual harassment to be a problem. Sexual teasing, ogling, and touching is ubiquitous enough that they think these types of behaviors are a normal part of everyday school experience.

Compounding the problem is the fact that gender-based violence is not limited to schools; it takes place in homes, on the Internet, at workplaces, and in the media. At times these types of abuses overlap, as we have seen with recent incidents of unwanted "sexting" among teens or stalking via social networking sites such as Facebook and Myspace. Women, girls, and LGBTQ people face violent and disrespectful treatment that is often considered socially acceptable. Many times, the sexual harassment of boys is ignored out of disbelief that a boy could be harassed by a girl, or it's downplayed as "boys will be boys." As a result, sexual harassment does not receive a lot of attention—but the personal and institutional consequences of ignoring this behavior are great.

Some young people find sexually inappropriate behavior to be "no big deal," but others disagree; for them, sexual harassment brings feelings of depression, fear, and insecurity. Nearly one in four (23 percent) participants said that he/she had personally been a victim of sexual harassment at school. We asked these students if the harassment impacted their ability to focus in school, and we provided them with an opportunity to write longer responses. The students' responses fell into three themes: depression, fear/insecurity, and feeling violated. Many participants said they felt sad and depressed after being sexually harassed. One participant told us, "I couldn't concentrate and kept crying for no reason." Another said, "My grades dropped and I was always depressed."

> **So the dean says that I know how young men think and I'm at fault for wearing an outfit that provoked that sort of attention, that I should have known better so he can't do anything about it! So, I decide to tell my friends and they're all like "Snitch . . ." and "Punk . . ." like I was wrong for telling because they'd kill for that attention because "he look mad good . . ." and "all he wanted to do was holla at you." Maybe I did want someone to tell me how nice I looked, just not the way he did.**
>
> **—Ariel, youth organizer**

Another theme that arose from the data was students' feelings of fear, insecurity, or post-traumatic stress after being harassed. Some students wrote that they were "scared to come to school" and "felt very unsafe." Others wrote that they couldn't stop thinking about the incident, and that they felt violated, "It kept flashing through my head" and "I got sick." Our research reveals the powerlessness students face when they experience gender-based violence.

We asked students to indicate whether they had ever reported sexual harassment, regardless of whether it happened to them directly. Almost all of the youth (97 percent) said they had not reported it. When participants were prompted to elaborate on their responses, several themes emerged, the most common being that sexual harassment was simply accepted as a part of what it meant to be at school. As one participant succinctly wrote, "It's normal at school now." Female students reported that sexual harassment took place in the most populated, interactive areas in schools; therefore, this behavior must be witnessed by other students. Coupled with the lack of reporting, this finding implies that students believe sexual harassment is routine and acceptable. One young person wrote, "It's not really sexual harassment. Students are just being playful." While another said, "I didn't see it as an issue because it was verbal and just joking." Others simply wrote, "It was not that serious" and "It wasn't that big of a deal."

Youth also told us they felt it was up to the people being harassed to report sexual harassment themselves. Many participants wrote, "It was none of [their] business" and that they "didn't want to get involved." They told us they felt peer pressure not to report sexual harassment if they witnessed it, and were teased when they did. One student wrote, "I got laughed at," and another told us, "They [peers] told me not to be a punk."

Students who indicated they had reported sexual harassment were asked to explain what happened afterward. The majority of students (52 percent) said that they did not know how students who sexually harassed others were dealt with at their school because there was no follow-up with them by school authorities. When asked what happened when they reported sexual harassment at school, some students responded, "Nothing," or "I have no idea," or suggested that the harasser was not reprimanded at all. "They did nothing."

Participants felt school authorities were unresponsive to their concerns, and some victims were made to feel they were to blame. One youth wrote, "They made me feel like I was the one who did something wrong." (Twenty-two percent who reported sexual harassment were further victimized.) Only 1.5 percent (or 18 out of 1,189) of participants wrote that the harasser was dealt with appropriately (e.g., the harasser was talked to by school staff and/or suspended).

Many students are unaware that there are policies protecting them and their classmates from sexual harassment. Fifty-seven percent of respondents said sexual harassment is "rarely" or "never" discussed in school. As stated before, students are unclear about which behaviors constitute sexual harassment infringements. They are unaware of how to go about report-ing incidents of sexual harassment, or that reporting is even an option.

Finding #3: youth want and need more education about sexual harassment.

When youth experience sexual harassment, they are more likely to tell a friend (48 percent) or a parent (43 percent) than they are to tell a teacher (34 percent). Fif-teen percent said they would do nothing. (The gender breakdown on this response is quite interesting, as 21 percent of males compared to 11 percent of females responded in this way.) When we asked students to write about their options for responding to sexual harassment, over a third of the responses involved physical violence. Youth wrote that they would "beat up," "punch," or "kill" the person who harassed them. An overwhelming number (85 percent) of students told us schools should provide more help for victims of sexual harassment. Compared with the number of stu-dents who claimed sexual harassment was "not a prob-lem" in their schools at the beginning of the survey, the number of students who believed that victims of sexual harassment needed more support was overwhelming. This shows that students saw sexual harassment as a serious issue after taking the survey.

Our findings reveal that students believe there isn't enough education about sexual harassment in schools and that this lack of knowledge results in students' tak-ing matters into their own hands, many times with poor and ineffective results. When asked what can be done about sexual harassment, youth recommended more discussion and education as well as more effective discipline and education for perpetrators. Participants wrote, "Inform people on how to avoid [sexual harassment] and punish those who do it," "Talk about it more and explain what it is," and "Make more known what the consequences are." Another told us that schools and community groups "should have workshops teaching students about sexual harassment." Some youth thought that "teachers should pay more attention" and suggested educating school staff, teachers, and authorities in addition to students about sexual harassment.

When young people are harassed and assaulted daily, they learn that they deserve this treatment; they learn to be silent about the violence they experience. Through these experiences, young women and LGBTQ youth especially are taught to put up with violent and destructive treatment because they have "no choice." The sense of powerlessness contributes to young people making unhealthy choices about their bodies, dropping out of school, or attempting suicide. Young men especially are trained to continue these behaviors, and witnesses are trained to stand idly by.

Young people in New York City public schools are not aware of sexual harassment policies in schools. Therefore, they turn to friends for support or to physical violence rather than reporting sexually inappropriate behavior to school authorities. According to the NYCDOE's website, a "Notice of Student Sexual Harassment Policy (CR A-831)" must be posted in each school, must list the staff member designated to receive reports of sexual harassment, and must include where a copy of the regulation and complaint form may be obtained. Additionally, the NYCDOE's sexual harassment brochure must be distributed to all students annually. It is clear from participants' responses that this is not happening. Students want and need more education, and we believe it is the Department of Education's responsibility to ensure that schools are complying with city regulations.

Today's heartbreaking climate of widespread youth suicides has led the US Department of Education's Office of Civil Rights to issue a letter to educators released on October 26, 2010.* The letter reinforces the need for uniform implementation of and compliance with Title IX of the Education Amendment. It also stresses that Title IX prohibits discrimination based solely on sexual orientation, thereby protecting LGBTQ students and educators from sexual harassment and gender-based harassment. This is the first time that the Office of Civil Rights has articulated the responsibilities that schools have to protect LGBTQ students and educators against gender-based harassment and violence. GGE has worked tirelessly to enforce support of and compliance with Title IX for the past ten years. The urgency to end gender-based violence and to promote social justice isn't new for GGE, and we are seizing this momentum of recent political support.

*http://www2.ed.gov/about/offices/list/ocr/letters/colleague-201010.pdf.

Conclusion
Joanne N. Smith

Girls for Gender Equity will celebrate its landmark tenth anniversary on September 11, 2011. As we move into our second decade of community service, GGE is at a pivotal tipping point in the organization's existence. This book is a milestone for us to reflect on and celebrate our impact to date. With that, GGE moves toward the next decade of our work. We're strategically building our capacity, upgrading our analysis and over the next ten years we will "go to scale" so our impact spans nationally and internationally. We predict we'll be members of the White House Council on Women and Girls as we're currently contributing to the larger dialogue redefining gender, challenging homophobia, and combating violence against women locally, nationally, and internationally. The world can no longer ignore that gender-based violence is a health, education, and economic-development issue that negatively affects our entire society. We are poised to act as experts, resources, and community voices as well as to benefit from the knowledge that others possess. GGE's work connects the abstract vision of gender justice movements to the concrete skills needed to evoke change daily.

Sisters in Strength's leadership of the Coalition for Gender Equity in Schools gives voice and backing to New York City's most vulnerable youth from underserved communities of color affected by the sexist, racist, and homophobic violence embedded in school culture. We make a sustained effort to incorporate parents and educators in order to fully embrace the communities this work affects. But we also prioritize youth leadership at all levels of coalition work, because they are the experts on the topic of school as well as the most important stakeholders in this activism.

We are designing culturally competent educational tools, such as a *Hey . . . Shorty!* workshop curriculum to accompany the documentary and Know Your Rights pamphlets that build a common language to discuss sexual harassment and gender-based violence in schools. These tools were drafted and edited by sixty-seven middle and high school-age students alongside

CGES protest against the DOE budget cuts.

community-based organizations. The New York Civil Liberties Union and CGES have embarked on a phone and letter-writing campaign to identify the Title IX coordinators assigned to individual schools citywide. The results of these findings will be brought to the NYCDOE in an effort to call attention to the poor enforcement of Title IX in New York City and demand that a mandated listing of the coordinators be added to schools' websites.

The SIS interns and I were transformed into more confident women, more socially aware, and more inspired to continue community organizing and social justice. I take my experiences with Sisters in Strength with me everywhere I go.
—Latosha, youth organizer

In 2009, CGES members secured a three-year grant from the Robert Wood Johnson Foundation: Peaceful Pathways—Reducing Exposure to Violence to sustain CGES's efforts. As we move into the 2010–2011 school year, this support allows us to build on our accomplishments and strengthen our four campaign objectives of youth leadership, education, advocacy, and replicability.

We will develop youth leadership throughout the city on sexual harassment and gender-based violence. The young people of CGES will regularly participate in monthly group facilitation and campaigns, and be trained for visible and influential leadership roles within CGES. We will increase parent and teacher membership to further foster intergenerational learning.

We will educate youth, parents, educators, and school communities about sexual harassment and provide them with tools to handle and prevent it. We will finalize and publish the *Hey . . . Shorty!* workshop curriculum for peer education to accompany the *Hey . . . Shorty!* documentary film and this book. CGES's youth from partner organizations will lead workshops at schools and at community-based organizations using multimedia teaching tools. NYCDOE schools will teach from the Know Your Rights pamphlet. Using video cameras, CGES will develop a youth-lead multimedia, strategic-communications plan with targeted messages on YouTube, social-networking sites, and cable TV.

> My experiences at GGE continue to impact my life. We took a topic that I thought was not so widespread and found out that so many more people deal with it. So opening up and talking about it showed that we are not alone in this world. If you've been hurt or abused, there are other people that also have the same experiences. It's only when you start talking about it and take a stand against it when some of the pain will subside and you can look at a stronger, brighter future.
>
> —Nadia, youth organizer

We will relentlessly advocate for a uniform implementation of Title IX, and new, comprehensive policies to address gender-based violence and discrimination in schools. We will follow up on recommendations given throughout the 2009–2010 school year at the NYCDOE Discipline Code hearing. We will further develop Sisters in Strength members' expertise on Title IX policy, and strategically align with mutually supportive organizations and coalitions who are advocating for changes to the New York City Discipline Code and to policies that continue to foster inequitable education.

Finally, we will develop the Sisters in Strength and CGES model to be used as a replicable strategy to make schools safer for all students and free of gender-based oppression. We'll continue to track CGES's progress and scope (evaluation tools include surveys, focus groups, anecdotal data, and continued participatory action research). We will develop and disseminate our most effective methods at local and national conferences, and broaden our scope as we travel nationally with this book.

The Dignity for All Students Act (DASA) was recently signed into New York State law, an enumerated, antibullying bill that includes protections from bullying and discrimination on the basis of sexual orientation, and gender identity and expression. New York has become the tenth state to enact an antibullying law that includes a list of characteristics most often targeted by bullies, which research shows is more effective than a general antibullying law. With the addition of DASA, there are now three legal mandates—Respect for All (New York City), Dignity for All Students Act (New York State), and Title IX (US)—that require a trained staff member in each school to receive reports of sexual harassment and bullying. DASA will be first implemented during the 2012-2013 school year, and GGE is part of the DASA Task Force. GGE's work to make New York City public schools safer is far from over. In fact, in many ways, after ten years, it has only just begun. Like most community organizing, our success is incremental, slow moving, and sometimes difficult to see. Our Sisters in Strength youth organizers, year after year, attest to our most definitive progress.

Appendixes

What is Sexual Harassment?

Does someone have to touch you for it to be sexual harassment? Do sexually suggestive words count? If someone is staring at your body, is it sexual harassment? Can a friend sexually harass you? What if it only happens once?

After ten years of doing work to prevent sexual harassment in the New York City public schools, we have come up with a rather broad working definition of sexual harassment: sexual harassment is any unwanted behavior or attention of a sexual nature that may or may not interfere with a person's ability to participate in or benefit from a school's programs or activities.

Identifying sexual harassment can be confusing. Sometimes we are unable to express exactly what we believe happened to us. We may be unsure of why it happened or whether what happened was okay, especially if the perpetrator is our friend. We may not understand why we feel embarrassed or uncomfortable. These are common questions and reactions that, unfortunately, don't have easy answers.

Although sexual harassment involves sexual behaviors, it's actually not about sex. People who harass others are acting in a way that communicates aggression, hostility, and a desire for control. They feel powerful by making someone, who they see as inferior, feel scared or uncomfortable. Sometimes they simply want attention. Regardless of their motivation, perpetrators of sexual harassment need to be stopped.

Some behaviors are severe enough that they only need to happen once to constitute sexual harassment. For example, if Student A gropes Student B's breasts, butt, or genitals in the hallway between classes without permission, this is clearly inappropriate and need not be repeated to be called sexual harassment. Another example of a clear case of sexual harassment is if someone says or writes lewd comments about a student, such as "Jen is a slut" or "Benjamin is a faggot." This creates a hostile environment for Jen and Benjamin that can interfere with their ability to learn.

However, if Student A asks Student B out on a date and Student B is not interested, this may be annoying, but it's not harassment if the behavior is not repeated. The bottom line is that if a behavior feels bad and makes you uncomfortable, you have the right to tell the person to stop. If they don't stop, you have the right to ask your school to intervene.

Sexual harassment affects our lives in profound ways because it grows out of larger forms of individual and institutional oppression that we experience as young people, women, people of color, immigrants, and members of the LGBTQ community. Achieving social justice is not just about race or class or gender or ability or nationality or religion. It's about all of those things at once, because, as Mahatma Gandhi famously said, "No one is free when others are oppressed."

Sexual harassment can include, but is not limited to:

Touching, pinching, or grabbing someone else's breasts, butt, or genitals

Touching, pinching, or grabbing your own breasts, butt, or genitals in front of others

Sexual comments, jokes, stories, song lyrics, or rumors

Gestures and facial expressions (e.g., winking or licking lips)

Inappropriate looks or staring at someone's body

Clothing pulled to reveal your body or someone else's body

Sexual pictures or drawings (e.g., a pornographic magazine)

Demands for sexual activity

Physical intimidation (e.g., standing too close to someone, following someone, blocking someone's way so they can't leave)

Cyberbullying (when the Internet, cell phones, or other devices are used to send or post text or images intended to hurt or embarrass another person) *

*National Crime Prevention Council definition of cyberbullying, www.ncpc.org/cyberbullying.

How to Stop Sexual Harassment

HOW TO RESPOND IN THE MOMENT

Tell the person to stop. Sometimes sexual harassment is the result of miscommunication, so if someone is making you uncomfortable, it's important to clearly establish your personal boundaries and comfort level. As directly and explicitly as possible, communicate that his/her behavior is offensive and unwanted. Figure out ahead of time which words would be the strongest to communicate your discomfort in a situation. Practice using your voice to deliver this message effectively. Some examples might include, "It makes me uncomfortable when you hug me. Please don't do it," or "Please don't ask me out again. I'm not interested."

Do not make excuses. It might seem easier to make excuses like, "I have a boyfriend," or "I have plans on Friday night." But these don't address the real issue and could encourage the harasser to persist. Hold the harasser accountable for his/her inappropriate behavior and identify that behavior as sexual harassment. Don't worry about hurting his/her feelings; he/she obviously isn't worried about hurting yours.

Your body language is an important tool for communication. Laughing or smiling can undermine what you are saying and communicate that you aren't serious. Sit or stand up straight, and look the harasser directly in the eye while speaking with a firm voice.

Remain firm and refuse to engage in a debate. Sometimes a harasser will make excuses for his/her behavior or try to convince you that he/she didn't mean to offend you. An argument can be a way for a harasser to maintain control and manipulate you into submitting to his/her desire.

Remain calm, composed, and nonviolent. Do not do anything that could jeopardize your safety or call your character into question. Unfortunately, victims of sexual harassment are unfairly scrutinized. Don't provide any ammunition that could be used against you.

Get away from the harasser as soon as you can. If the person continues to harass you after you've attempted to clearly communicate your desire for him/her to stop, there could be a larger problem involving discrimination or abuse. You may need to seek assistance from a bystander. Once you are safe, ask an authority figure for help.

HOW TO RESPOND AFTER BEING SEXUALLY HARASSED

Sometimes individuals are unable to respond to sexual harassment when it is happening. People don't always have the energy or are not always prepared to address an inappropriate comment in the moment. An incident could catch a person off guard, or he/she might be too scared to speak up at the time that he/she was harassed. **Always trust your instincts when it comes to your safety.**

You have a right to speak up for yourself. It takes strength and conviction to stand up for yourself, and the more you do the more powerful your words will become. If you aren't comfortable confronting your harasser face-to-face, write him/her a letter. Tell your side of the events that took place, including how the incident made you feel at the time, and if it affected you negatively afterward (e.g., inability to concentrate, feelings of depression).

Demand that the harasser stop the inappropriate behavior. The letter can be delivered personally, by a trusted friend or witness, or by an authority figure. Keep a dated copy of the letter for yourself.

HOW TO RESPOND WHEN YOU ARE A WITNESS TO SEXUAL HARASSMENT

Refuse to be a passive bystander when you've witnessed harassment. Speaking out against harassment contributes to your own safety. Sometimes when someone is being sexually harassed, he/she is too embarrassed or shocked to respond on his/her own. That person may need for someone to intervene. If you observe someone being sexually harassed, ask if he/she needs help and how you might be able to help. You could say, "You look uncomfortable. Is there some way that I can help?" Tell the victim that he/she does not need to tolerate abusive behavior. Encourage the victim to stand up to his/her harasser and offer your support by volunteering to be a witness.

Stay calm while speaking directly and firmly, and help the victim leave the situation as quickly as possible. Being loud could draw attention to the situation, which may embarrass or anger the harasser. These emotions could escalate the situation and create unnecessary danger. Offer to escort the victim to his/her destination.

Tell the victim that he/she is not to blame for the harassment. Many people believe that they have done something to cause the harassment. The witness should assure the victim that he/she is not to blame. The witness could say, "That person was out of line. You deserve to be treated with respect."

File a report. This can be done whether or not the victim comes forward. It's not unreasonable for you to want for your school to be a safe environment for all students. If another person's behavior seems suspicious, you have a right to call attention to it in order to create a harassment-free environment.

HOW TO RECORD INCIDENTS OF SEXUAL HARASSMENT

Whether you are being personally harassed or witnessing incidents of harassment, write down what you saw or heard as soon as possible. Take notes every time it happens. The Five W's below are a good guideline:

WHO—Who was involved? If you know their names, write them down. If you don't, write down a description of their physical appearance including age, hair color, height, build, and clothing.

WHAT—What happened? Note the exact details of the incident, including specifics about the harasser's body language, the exact words he/she used, and if there was any physical contact—exactly what happened.

WHEN—What was the date and time of the incident? Even if you don't look at a clock immediately afterward, write down the approximate time that the incident occurred. You could write down, "Between second and third period," or "After school before the buses left," or "12:37 p.m." Write down whatever you know.

WHERE—Where did it happen? Was it on the second floor of your school? In the cafeteria? In front of locker number 312?

WITNESSES—Were there any witnesses to the incident? Who were they? Did a security guard walk by? A teacher? Maybe another student? Was a group of friends there? Write down their names if you know them or physical descriptions if you don't.

Having a record of a sexual harassment incident will give you clarity when you tell your allies and the authority figures at your school. It will help you keep the facts straight, give you a place to vent your frustrations, and decrease your self-doubt. Document the effects of the harassment on your physical and emotional well-being and your school performance. Keep a journal that includes any negative feelings that are the result of the harassment (e.g., feelings of depression, an inability to complete schoolwork, etc.). Keep copies of tests and papers that may have suffered as a result of the sexual harassment. If you are being harassed by a teacher, document any threats or demands he/she may impose on you, such as threatening to giving you a poor grade or taking away a privilege. This type of evidence strengthens a report of sexual harassment.

HOW TO REPORT SEXUAL HARASSMENT

The first step is to know your rights as a student. Every school in the United States is required to have policies and reporting procedures that cover sexual harassment. It is the school's responsibility to make sure those policies and procedures are readily available to students. Solicit the help of a parent or family member who will support you in this process. Find out who is responsible—the principal, vice principal, guidance counselor—for handling the sexual harassment complaints at your school.

HOW TO COPE WITH FEELINGS

Sexual harassment can be traumatic. Experiencing sexual harassment, especially in silence, can lead to many negative feelings. It's important to talk to others about your experience. Most harassers have more than one victim. Speaking up can help you gain the support you need to protect yourself and others. You may not have the power to stop sexual harassment on your own, but by telling others you gain support and power in numbers, which could help you to figure out the best response together and take action.

In our research we found that students who experienced sexual harassment said it impacted their ability to focus in school for a variety of reasons. Some felt the effects of sexual harassment as depression: "I couldn't concentrate and kept crying for no reason," or "My grades dropped and I was always depressed." Others experienced fear and insecurity: "I was scared to come to school" or "I felt very unsafe." Still others felt violated: "It was disturbing and kept flashing through my head," or "I felt violated." Additional negative effects that students expressed after being sexually harassed included: feeling bad about themselves (e.g., their body, their intelligence, their ability to be respected); feeling guilt, blaming themselves for the experience; replaying the incident over and over in their heads; being scared to go back to the location of the incident; being afraid to interact with their harasser again; questioning their ability to stand up for themselves.

In cases of severe emotional distress, speaking to a mental health professional who understands how the experience of sexual harassment may impact one's psychological well-being may be necessary. Remember that sexual harassment is not your fault. Sexual harassment is a behavior that is imposed on the victim, not one that the victim asks for.

Self-defense classes offer safe spaces for you to regain your confidence, practice using your voice, and learn how to protect your body from harm. Self-defense classes are often offered free to women and LGBTQ people at local gyms or community centers. Self-defense may sound like it involves violence, but there are many forms that do not involve physical action. The first method of defense is using your voice. If you are still uncomfortable or unsafe after telling the person to stop, removing yourself from the situation is the next strategy of self-defense. Using physical techniques is always the last resort.

HOW TO IDENTIFY ADULT ALLIES INSIDE AND OUTSIDE OF SCHOOL

An adult ally is someone who lends their support to a young person who has been the victim of sexual harassment. Allies listen to and trust young people's experiences, opinions, and ideas. Adult allies recognize that young people are the experts in their own experience and know that adults do not have all the answers. An adult ally values the experiences and opinions of youth. They offer guidance and assistance, but do not force their own judgments and ideas on youth. An adult ally works with young people to prevent and respond to sexual harassment.

Getting to know teachers, counselors, and administrators you feel comfortable with, even if they don't teach or counsel you personally, can be extremely beneficial. You can also find adult allies in your family. Many of you have aunts, uncles, and grandparents you trust.

Adult allies are in a unique position to assist young people in promoting and working toward social change. They can raise awareness among adults about age bias that functions to normalize discrimination against young people. They can challenge and educate other adults about the privilege their age automatically brings them.

Having adult allies is important for youth. They can provide resources, information, and access to solutions that cannot be supplied by other young people. If the adult ally is in the school, they can increase their supervision over the harasser. Adult allies will respect you, listen to you, and advocate on your behalf. All of this is vital when something inappropriate or dangerous happens.

Unfortunately many school officials see sexual harassment as typical of youth. They believe sexually harassing others and being sexually harassed are inevitable. Many of the same adults have been victims of or engaged in sexual harassment themselves, and are unaware or uneducated about the issue. This doesn't make them inherently bad, but it means you may have to search for an empathetic adult who understands sexual harassment and sees it as behavior that should not be tolerated.

Here are some characteristics of an adult ally:

— Believes the victim
— Doesn't blame the victim
— Takes the victim's issue seriously and doesn't downplay its importance or impact
— Intervenes when sexual harassment or age discrimination occurs
— Is willing to talk with and listen to young people
— Is open to criticism (especially from youth) about their own biases, shortcomings, or lack of understanding as a result of their age
— Recognizes their own limitations and takes responsibility for their mistakes
— Treats everyone with dignity and respect regardless of age, gender, sexual orientation, race, ability, etc.

— Has antidiscrimination rules for their classroom and incorporates anti-oppression lessons into their teaching
— Helps students organize against discrimination (e.g., poster campaigns, school assemblies, after-school groups)

HOW TO RESPOND TO A YOUNG PERSON WHO HAS BEEN SEXUALLY HARASSED

Sexual harassment is not an easy topic to discuss, but it's important to remember that as uncomfortable as you may be with the topic, a victim of sexual harassment is probably much more uncomfortable. When a young person comes to you to talk about the incident, he/she is expressing that you are an adult whom he/she trusts. The young person has taken a brave step, and it is important that you handle the situation with patience, sensitivity, and understanding while refraining from negative judgments about those involved. Listen to the young person and answer the questions that come up to the best of your ability. If you need assistance with factual information, don't be afraid to say that you don't know and take time to utilize books, websites, or other people as resources. Remember to make it clear that the victim is not at fault for the harassment he/she has experienced.

Depending on the severity of the situation, and what the young person wants to do, school officials may need to be notified. The student may need your assistance in explaining what happened to school officials. The events should be recorded in writing with as much detail as possible, including any witness accounts of the incident. (A good guideline is the Five W's. See How to Record Incidents of Sexual Harassment, page 146.) It is also important to let the young person know that you will support him/her and follow through with what you both agree upon as the next steps, such as confronting the harasser and/or reporting the incident.

Keep in mind that girls and LGBTQ youth can be especially vulnerable to sexual harassment, and that its effect on their confidence, self-esteem, ability to concentrate, stress level, school participation, and social development can be devastating and long-lasting. (See How to Cope with Feelings, page 148.) The feelings the victim is dealing with do not always end once the incident is addressed. Continue to take time to ask the young person how you can support him/her.

RESPONDING TO A YOUNG PERSON WHO HAS BEEN ACCUSED OF SEXUAL HARASSMENT

Don't assume a young person's innocence or guilt. Let them explain the incident and ask nonjudgmental questions. (An example of a judgmental question is "Don't you know better than this?") A person accused of sexual harassment may say they didn't mean to do so, and they may not understand why their actions have been interpreted as hurtful. It is important to explain that sexual harassment is not simply a matter of the harasser's intention, but is determined by the perception of the victim. If the harasser made the victim feel uncomfortable or unsafe, it is harassment.

Growing up, young people receive mixed messages about how to interact with one another from their families, their peers, and the media. Sometimes these messages tell them that girls and women are inferior to boys and men, and that LGBTQ individuals are abnormal, which provides an excuse for treating these groups poorly. The bottom line is that everyone deserves to be respected. To help the young person better understand what has happened and why, ask them some evaluating questions:

— Would you engage in the same behavior in front of people you respect (e.g., parents or teachers)?
— Would it be okay if someone else did the same thing to your brother or sister?
— Would you continue the behavior if you knew it made the person uncomfortable?
— How do you think the victim feels?
— How can you rectify this situation?

For more resources, visit ggenyc.org.

STRATEGIES FOR PREVENTION FOR PARENTS, SCHOOL STAFF, AND STUDENTS

Sexual harassment is not so different from other bias-based behaviors, including racism and homophobia. Although individuals can and should stand up to perpetrators of sexual harassment, the strength of the effort can be increased by coming together to organize and advocate for one's rights and the rights of others. Public schools are supposed to be welcoming, safe places for all students, and people must work together toward this common goal to ensure that is the case.

HOW PARENTS CAN PREVENT SEXUAL HARASSMENT IN SCHOOLS

Parents of students who are sexually harassed can feel powerless, and being a part of a group effort to address the issue can combat this feeling of frustration. The first step to working together is having a willingness to work *with* the school to make it a safer environment for students. Parents can do this by seeking out opportunities to join leadership groups, like the parent-led Mother's Agenda NY, CGES, or even the Parent-Teacher Association. If there isn't a group you feel is sufficiently meeting the school's safety needs, you can always start an anti-discrimination group yourself for parents, teachers, students, or any combination of the three. Acting as a leader in your student's school sets a positive example for your child in teaching him or her how to stand up for his or her rights, showing him or her that perpetrators—whether individuals or institutions—can be held accountable, and demonstrating that change is possible. You have the right and responsibility to make sure your children are protected from violence and harassment at school.

We talked earlier about the reasons parents may not be able to participate in leadership groups, so here are some strategies parents can implement in their daily lives to help prevent sexual harassment in schools:

— Model appropriate behavior. Refuse to laugh at sexist, homophobic, or transphobic comments and jokes. Have discussions with your child about why those things are not funny.

— Encourage your child to speak up for him or herself. Promoting self-confidence in a child is the first step to prevent him or her from becoming victims of sexual harassment or other types of abuse.

— Encourage your child to discuss school life with you, including grades, sports, extracurricular activities, and friends. Let your child know you are interested and available to talk, no matter what the topic.

— Talk to your child about why prejudice and discrimination are hurtful and correct any misconceptions they may have about other groups.

— Use language that is inclusive of both genders and avoids stereotyping individuals based on gender, sexual orientation, race, ethnicity, or other characteristics.

— Suggest and seek out ways your child can participate in leadership training opportunities at school or elsewhere.

— Raise your child's awareness of other people's feelings. Fostering a sense of respect, empathy, and compassion will help prevent your child from hurting others.

— Talk to your child about healthy friendships and dating relationships.

— Take advantage of "teachable moments." When an incident of sexual harassment occurs in your presence (whether in the school, on the street, or in a store), seize the opportunity to raise your child's awareness about sexual harassment and openly communicate to your child that such behavior is unacceptable, hurtful, and illegal.

— Request a copy of your child's school's sexual harassment policy. Keep it on hand as a reference. If any part is unclear to you, make an appointment with an administrator to clarify any questions or concerns you may have about the policy or reporting procedures.

— If your child's school does not have a sexual harassment policy or has a policy that is confusing or inaccessible, talk to the school administrator or a school board representative.

— Discuss the school's antidiscrimination policy with your children. Let them know that you are aware sexual harassment is a problem in schools, and that you are available to talk about it.

— Ask your child's school to put sexual harassment on the agenda for parent-teacher meetings or events, as well as parent discussions. If you are qualified, offer to lead a discussion group or series of talks for the parent community.

— Create and distribute materials to help other parents and their children discuss issues like sex education, gender equity, and sexism.

HOW SCHOOL STAFF CAN PREVENT SEXUAL HARASSMENT IN SCHOOLS

It is important for schools to address sexual harassment for several reasons: (1) It is against the law. (2) It can be costly to a school or district. (3) It makes learning in schools very difficult and sometimes impossible. (4) Everyone involved has the potential to be hurt in some way (the victim, the harasser, bystanders, school staff, and others). Students and school staff must be able to feel safe in their schools and maintaining a safe school environment is everyone's responsibility. By law, every school receiving federal funding must have an official policy for sexual harassment, and if a school doesn't have an official policy, or does not follow it, it is breaking the law.

Teachers are the front line of defense for students in preventing sexual harassment in schools, and advocating on students' behalf can sometimes endanger one's position. Here are some strategies we suggest you cautiously use to be an ally to your students:

— Become or identify an adult ally for students who can handle sexual harassment issues that concern students. This person can serve as a liaison between students and administrators on sexual harassment concerns (as opposed to a person who receives formal complaints). This signals to students that there is someone they can talk to who understands.

— Talk to other staff members about sexual harassment prevention and form a coalition of sexual harassment advocates in your school who support the students and each other in creating a safer environment.

— Include information about sexual harassment as a part of every classroom's code of conduct for students. Hold students accountable to this code of conduct.

— Reach out to students who are frequently picked

on or made to feel badly about themselves. Let them know you care about them. Encourage them to stand up to this form of aggression and stand up to it yourself as well.

— Model the behavior you want to instill in young people. Never tolerate behaviors and comments by students or colleagues that have a tone of gender insensitivity or disrespect. Speak up when students or colleagues stereotype males, females, and LGBTQ people or make discriminatory jokes or comments. Ignoring actions or remarks that trivialize or put down girls, women, and LGBTQ people communicates that such put-downs are acceptable, feeds into sexual harassment, and suggests that females and LGBTQ people are inferior and undeserving of protection.

— Take advantage of "teachable moments." When an incident of sexual harassment occurs in your presence, seize the opportunity to raise awareness about sexual harassment and openly communicate to your students that such behavior is unacceptable, hurtful, and illegal.

— Give your students an anonymous survey about their experiences of sexual harassment in school that gains information about students' perceptions of the problem and the impact sexual harassment can have on students. Then share the results with school administrators to raise consciousness about the problem.

— Empower students to speak up if they are sexually harassed. Advise students to tell the

harasser, firmly and assertively, to stop. Point out that body language and facial expressions are as important as words in delivering this message.
— Use prevention posters that inform students and staff about sexual harassment and make sure they are prominently displayed throughout the school.
— Check restrooms periodically for graffiti of a sexual nature or that spreads sexual rumors about students.
— Ask the administrators at your school to hold an assembly about sexual harassment and to bring in educators who are qualified to speak to each class about the topic.
— Check to see if there is a sexual harassment policy and Title IX coordinator at your school. If there isn't one, find out who you can speak to in order to advocate for one without endangering your position. You can even volunteer to write the policy and grievance procedures yourself, and include the students in the process of doing so.
— Have regular contact with parents, and include them in any incidents that occur, particularly if disciplinary action is taken.

HOW STUDENTS CAN PREVENT SEXUAL HARASSMENT IN SCHOOLS

Many of us—especially women, people of color, LGBTQ people, those who are differently abled, immigrants, and people living in low-income communities—are taught to be silent about the injustice that we endure. We are taught that speaking up for ourselves and our communities will bring more harm than good, and while it is true that advocating for our rights is full of disappointments and hardships, remaining silent will never bring about change. Students have the power to speak out about sexual harassment and join forces with other students, parents, and teachers in order to raise awareness and change the climate of their schools to one of respect and safety.

— Educate yourself about sexual harassment, especially your school's sexual harassment policy. Know what kinds of behaviors are prohibited in your school, what the consequences are for these behaviors, and how to report infractions.

— If your school doesn't have a sexual harassment policy or formal reporting procedures, find out who you need to speak with to advocate for them to be instituted at your school.

— Never tolerate behaviors and comments by other students or teachers that have a tone of gender insensitivity or disrespect. Speak up when people stereotype males, females, and LGBTQ people or make discriminatory jokes or comments. Ignoring actions or remarks that trivialize or put down girls, women, and LGBTQ people communicates that such put-downs are acceptable, feeds into sexual harassment, and suggests that females and LGBTQ people are inferior and undeserving of protection.

— Start a student group that fights discrimination

in your school. You may even recruit a teacher to sponsor the group.

— It's important to figure out not only what to do for yourself, but also how you can empower others. Lead a discussion about sexual harassment with your peers or speak about it at a school assembly.

Myths about Sexual Harassment

MYTH: Sexual harassment is the same thing as flirting.

FACT: They are not the same thing. Sexual harassment is an *unwanted* behavior while flirting is a *wanted* behavior. Here are some ways to tell the difference:

Flirting	Sexual Harassment
Feels good	Feels uncomfortable
You enjoy it	You feel ashamed
Motivated by attraction	Motivated by power
Shared	One-sided
Flattering	Humiliating

MYTH: All perpetrators of sexual harassment are male.

FACT: Most harassers are male, but the truth is that boys *and* girls can sexually harass another person regardless of their sex. This means that victims and perpetrators can be male or female. Boys can sexually harass both girls *and* boys, and girls can sexually harass both boys *and* girls.

MYTH: You can only be sexually harassed by someone close to your age.

FACT: Sexual harassment doesn't just happen among your peers. It can also involve adults. Sometimes teachers, administrators, counselors, and other adults in the school may sexually harass students. This also means that students can sexually harass adults.

MYTH: If girls wear sexy clothes or play around with boys, they're asking to be harassed.

FACT: People sexually harass others to make themselves feel more powerful. Nothing someone says, does, or wears makes sexual harassment their fault. Girls and boys should have the right to wear whatever they want and be safe from sexual harassment.

MYTH: Girls make up stories about being sexually harassed because they want attention or revenge.

FACT: Sexual harassment is a frequent occurrence in the lives of all students, but especially for girls. Research shows that most girls don't file complaints even when they are justified in doing so. False complaints are extremely rare because reporting sexual harassment is difficult and the process can be very hostile to the woman making the complaint. Also, being identified as a victim of sexual harassment is a humiliating experience for most women. If someone tells you they have been sexually harassed, it is very important to believe them.

MYTH: If you don't mean to make someone uncomfortable, it isn't sexual harassment.

FACT: Intention is only part of the picture, and a person can sexually harass someone else without intending to or knowing it, but this is still sexual harassment! Remember that sexual harassment is determined by the way the victim feels. If your behavior makes them feel uncomfortable or unsafe, it is sexual harassment.

MYTH: Everyone is comfortable with the same types of physical contact.

FACT: It is important to keep in mind that everyone's comfort with physical contact, like hugging or hand-holding, and personal space is different. Comfort with physical contact and personal space is determined by one's culture, family dynamics, and trust of others with whom one has a relationship. When you are unsure about how someone else feels, ask them.

MYTH: If I see someone else being harassed, I do not have to report it.

FACT: If you witness sexual harassment, it is your responsibility to report it. It is up to all of us to keep our school and community safe.

MYTH: If being sexually harassed were serious enough, the person who was harassed would report it.

FACT: Sometimes people who have been harassed are embarrassed or scared to tell. They may feel like they are the only person to whom this has happened or think it was their fault. They may need a friend to help them report it.

MYTH: Sexual harassment is just harmless fun. It doesn't really hurt anybody.

FACT: Sexual harassment is serious, and it can be very harmful. There are many physical and psychological effects for people who are sexually harassed, such as a loss of trust in people, feeling bad about themselves, making bad grades, and even getting physically sick. Perpetrators of sexual harassment often use the behavior as a means to express power, control, and sometimes hostility toward women.

MYTH: There are no serious punishments for sexual harassment.

FACT: A student can be suspended, removed from sports teams, and in some cases, expelled from school for sexually harassing someone else.

MYTH: The best way to stop sexual harassment is to ignore it.

FACT: Ignoring sexual harassment will not make it go away; in fact, perpetrators often interpret silence as an indication that the behavior is enjoyed and encouraged, which can result in the harassment getting worse. If you are a victim of sexual harassment, the first thing you should do is firmly tell the person to stop. If they don't stop, you should get away from them and tell an adult whom you trust in your school.

Sexual Harassment Quiz

Can you tell the difference between wanted and unwanted actions? Which scenarios do you believe are sexual harassment?

(A) Dawn asks Chris on a date, and he happily accepts.
(B) Nick pulls Jonathan's pants down at recess in front of their friend Michael.
(C) Anna and Emily like to hold hands when they walk to class.
(D) Maya keeps bugging Taylor for a date after he says no many times.
(E) Coach Brady offers to let Keisha skip gym class if she gives him a kiss on the cheek.

Answers
(A) No, because Dawn wants to go out on a date with Chris, and Chris wants to go out on a date with Dawn.
(B) Yes, because Jonathan does not want his pants pulled down, and Nick embarrassed Jonathan. (Bonus Question: How many people are being sexually harassed? Answer: two. Jonathan is being harassed because his clothes are being pulled down to show his body. Michael is being harassed because he is being forced to see Jonathan's body.
(C) No, because both Anna and Emily like to hold hands. However, this may still be inappropriate for the school environment.

(D) Yes, because Maya is not respecting Taylor when he tells her no.

(E) Yes, because a teacher should never make a sexual request of a student for any reason, as it is an abuse of his or her authority. This is an example of quid pro quo sexual harassment.

Sexual Harassment Survey

Thank you for taking our survey about sexual harassment* in schools. We are trying to find out about the experiences that students have. Your responses are important to us. All of your answers are *anonymous* and *confidential*!

1. **What is your gender?**
   - ◯ Male
   - ◯ Female
   - ◯ Other (*please specify*)

   _____

2. **What is your race/ethnicity?**

   _____

   Age? _____

3. **What school do you attend?**

   _____

* *Sexual harassment* is any unwanted behavior of a sexual nature

4. **Do you think sexual harassment is a problem in your school?**
   - ○ Yes
   - ○ No

5. **Have you been sexually harassed at your school?**
   - ○ Yes
   - ○ No

6. **How often are students (including yourself) sexually harassed at your school?**
   (*choose one answer*)
   - ○ Daily
   - ○ 2–3 times a week
   - ○ Once a week
   - ○ 2–3 times a month
   - ○ Once a month
   - ○ A few times a year
   - ○ Never

7. **Ways that students are sexually harassed at your school include** (*choose all that apply*):
   - ○ Pressure for sex or sexual activity
   - ○ Touching, pinching, or brushing against a person sexually and on purpose
   - ○ Leaning over or cornering a person
   - ○ Sexually suggestive looks, gestures, or body language (examples: licking lips, moving hips in a "humping" motion)

- ○ Letters, phone calls, or Internet communication (email, Myspace) of a sexual nature
- ○ Pressure for dates
- ○ Sexual teasing, jokes, remarks, or questions (examples: calling a person a "slut" or "fag"; telling someone they have a nice body)
- ○ Whistles, calls, hoots, or yells of a sexual nature
- ○ Sexually explicit pictures or music on cell phones or other electronic devices
- ○ Forced sexual activity
- ○ Other (*please specify*)

_____

8. **How often do the following people *sexually harass others* in your school?**

(*choose one answer for each category*)

FREQUENTLY	SOMETIMES	RARELY	NEVER	
○	○	○	○	Male student
○	○	○	○	Female student
○	○	○	○	Classroom teacher
○	○	○	○	Substitute teacher
○	○	○	○	Gym teacher
○	○	○	○	Security guard
○	○	○	○	Principal/Vice Principal
○	○	○	○	Custodian
○	○	○	○	Other _____

9. How often are the following people sexually harassed in your school?

(*choose one answer for each category*)

FREQUENTLY	SOMETIMES	RARELY	NEVER	
O	O	O	O	Male students
O	O	O	O	Female students
O	O	O	O	Gay/Lesbian/Bisexual students
O	O	O	O	Transgender students

10. How often does sexual harassment happen at these places in your school?

(*choose one answer for each category*)

FREQUENTLY	SOMETIMES	RARELY	NEVER	
O	O	O	O	Locker room
O	O	O	O	Library
O	O	O	O	Security Station/Scanning
O	O	O	O	Staircase
O	O	O	O	Classroom
O	O	O	O	Hallway
O	O	O	O	Lunchroom/Cafeteria
O	O	O	O	After school
O	O	O	O	Outside on school property

11. Have you ever reported sexual harassment at your school?

- O Yes (if yes, answer question 11a)
- O No (if no, answer question 11b)

11a. What happened when you reported it?

_____

_____

_____

_____

11b. Why have you never reported it?
(*choose all that apply*)

○ I tried to get help, but was ignored by school staff.

○ I have never seen staff stop sexual harassment in the past.

○ I have never seen someone being sexually harassed.

○ I don't know how to report it.

○ Other (*please specify*)

_____

_____

12. If I were sexually harassed at school, I would . . .
(*choose all that apply*)

○ Tell a friend
○ Tell my parent/caregiver
○ Tell a teacher
○ Mope around
○ Drop out
○ Nothing
○ Other (*please specify*)

_____

_____

13. Has sexual harassment ever impacted your ability to focus in school?

○ Yes (*if yes, answer question 13a*)
○ No (*if no, go to question 14*)

13a. Please explain:

_____

_____

_____

_____

14. **Sexual harassment is discussed in schools . . .**
    - ◯ All the time
    - ◯ Sometimes
    - ◯ Rarely
    - ◯ Never

15. **Do you believe that schools should provide more help for victims of sexual harassment?**
    - ◯ Yes
    - ◯ No

16. **Most often, how are students who sexually harass others dealt with by staff (teachers, principal, counselor) in your school?**
    (*choose one answer*)
    - ◯ Given detention
    - ◯ Suspended or expelled from school
    - ◯ Sat down and talked to
    - ◯ Parent/caregiver called
    - ◯ Nothing happens to them
    - ◯ Police report is filed
    - ◯ I don't know
    - ◯ Other (*please specify*)

    _____

    _____

17. **What is the official policy on what should happen when incidents of sexual harassment happen in school?**

(*write only if you know*)

_____

_____

_____

_____

18. **I blame _____ the most for sexual harassment happening in schools.**

(*choose one answer*)

○ Department of Education
○ Principal
○ Students
○ Teachers
○ Myself
○ Other (*please specify*)

_____

_____

19. **What can people do to prevent sexual harassment from happening in schools?**

_____

_____

_____

_____

The Framework of GGE

GGE's work is dedicated to the unrealized feminists and activists who had no idea that there was power in their voices. It is also for the girls whose only example of leadership had been Angela Davis, and who then found their own innate leadership skills to facilitate workshops, or stand up for bullied classmates. We feel absolutely privileged to educate, support, and provide space for the feminists, activists, and changemakers who are helping to mold a world where gender justice is a reality.

Vision

GGE envisions a society with optimal physical, economic, educational, and social systems to foster the growth and fulfillment of all its members. To that end, we will provide programs that develop strengths, skills, and self-sufficiency in girls and women and help them make meaningful choices in their lives with minimum opposition and maximum community support. We will undertake organizing campaigns to achieve safety and equality in the social, political, educational, athletic, economic, health, and media worlds of the smaller and larger communities in which girls and women live and work.

Programs and Campaigns

GGE is the umbrella organization for three core programs and multiyear campaigns. Utilizing the principles laid out in our four-pronged advocacy and direct service model, GGE's programs and campaigns include:

1. **Urban Leaders Academy** is a holistic after-school program designed to help middle school students, ages eleven to fifteen, achieve academic excellence, explore career education, and maintain healthy lifestyles.

2. **Community Organizing** mobilizes youth and adults toward advocating for sustained change in their communities through educational campaigns, research, and direct action. Examples include Sisters in Strength, a paid community organizing internship for high school women of color, ages sixteen to nineteen, who receive advocacy training to act as peer mentors and tutors to middle school students in the Urban Leaders Academy, and the Coalition for Gender Equity in Schools (CGES) a citywide collaboration of New York City youth, parents, educators, activists, and community-based organizations committed to lending their expertise and resources to end sexual harassment and make public schools safer for all students.

3. **Health and Fitness Programs** help level the playing field in New York City schools and community-based organizations by coordinating

girls' participation in equitable sports teams, self-determination groups, and informative health workshops featuring harm-reduction strategies and reproductive justice education to promote awareness and healthy social development in preadolescent youngsters.

GGE's Four-Pronged Strategies

Intentionally interwoven throughout GGE's programs and campaigns are multifaceted strategies of intergenerational practice, a youth development model, interagency collaborations, and social justice curricula that help move GGE closer to our mission.

I. Since its inception, GGE has relied on our intergenerational and collaborative approach to movement building. A strategic approach to sustainable development, we call it "common sense survival" for a grassroots organization on a shoestring budget determined to mobilize community members while simultaneously leading three core programs for six hundred youth each year.

With only five full-time staff members, ten paid youth organizers, and standard overhead and program costs, GGE has been tremendously successful in leveraging community resources, from asking local businesses for in-kind donations to creating linkages with like-minded organizations willing to barter services, guest speakers, and space. However, our most valuable secret to successful foundation building is our agency structure of internships and volunteerism. Since 2001, GGE has provided six- to nine-month internships for high school, college, and graduate school students to develop organizing campaigns and programs. Through this internship, our core values include the holistic development of young people's leadership, critical thinking, transferable employment, and educational skills.

Our very first intern, Heather Burack, was placed with us as a first-year masters of social work student while I was in my second year of graduate school and before GGE even had a main office. Thank goodness Heather was willing to do whatever was necessary to deliver amazing programming for the girls, from working in her car while traveling from Brownsville to Bushwick schools, to leading self-determination groups for girls and parent workshops, to meeting with our undergraduate and high school interns as a task supervisor and mentor. The list of creative ways we have worked together is endless. Clearly, this was not an ideal situation at the beginning, but after ten years, over one hundred and thirty interns, and five hundred volunteers, GGE has developed a formula for recruiting talented people. It works like this: Throughout the year, but heavily from May through September, GGE posts online internship descriptions and sends placement requests to the field office of local college and graduate schools. This results in a team of four to eight interns who are then trained and supervised to co-lead programs and workshops, develop curricula, fundraise, secure linkages, create marketing material, and counsel youth between fourteen and twenty-one hours a week throughout the academic year.

To maintain the integrity of our programs, we bring

on interns ready to work on social justice issues pertinent to underserved communities of color, such as sexism, racism, homophobia, transphobia, reproductive injustice, gentrification, classism, and food injustice. The interns focus on the intersection of these "isms," which influence their own lives daily. Beginning with an orientation, the interns continue to receive training throughout the school year to further develop their social justice analysis, reflect on their own strengths as organizers, and garner tools that allow them to strategically lead as agents of change.

II. Our Youth Development Model is a working model adapted from Erik Erikson's psychosocial theory of development that considers a psychosocial theory of identity formation when exploring relationships between identity, agency, power, and cultural worlds of practice. Rooted in the desire to promote the optimal development of youth, this model provides youth with opportunities to: cultivate secure and stable relationships with caring peers and adults; be in safe, supportive environments with peers; develop relevant life skills; contribute to their communities; feel competent by highlighting effort rather than competition; and try new challenges. GGE encourages participants to: identify barriers to self-determination as young people of color; think critically about their role, and the roles of others, in systems of oppression; recognize these systems within their communities; and understand that it is possible to change oppressive, systemic structures. This model is composed of the following six overlapping components:

1. **Social Growth and Identity**: youth explore the concept of identity, develop social skills, grapple with moral issues, embrace physical changes, and build character in relation to self and the larger community, through a broad range of enrichment and support activities.
2. **Consciousness Raising**: challenging oneself and influencing others to think critically about systems of oppression, and the roles individuals and communities play in these systems.
3. **Education and Career**: promote cross-disciplinary academic excellence and exposure to nontraditional career goals.
4. **Health and Fitness**: building nutrition and fitness awareness and practice.
5. **Youth Leadership**: playing an active role in self-determination, which in turn has an impact on the community at large.
6. **Community Organizing for Social Justice**: building organizing skills and implementing strategies that mobilize the community to change gender, race, and class dynamics for people of color living in urban communities.

III. Our Interagency Model is a simple model for fostering agency collaborations with other nonprofit organizations that benefits all agencies involved, and eliminates the roadblocks that prevent effectiveness. Staff practice in-house program collaborations to reach overlapping program goals.

IV. GGE's Social Justice Curricula are developed in-house with youth, parents, educators, and staff. These culturally competent educational tools intentionally teach for social justice and incorporate our aforementioned multipronged approach to our work. These curricula include: Gender Respect Workshop series; Urban Leaders Academy service learning; Hey, Shorty! workshop curriculum and documentary.

Five Ways to Support Our Work

1

Support us and ask five friends to do the same! Your generosity is compounded when you ask others to support the work of GGE. Visit our donation page at ggenyc.org to make your secure donation now.

2

Give supplies. Drop off new items such as backpacks, office supplies, alarm clocks, laptops, and bedding for our amazing young women going off to college. Help prepare them to succeed.

3

Matching. Do you work for a company with a matching donor program? Set up a presentation to share our work with your team.

4

Host a party. Contact us to present GGE to your next dinner, party, or gathering. Tell your friends why you support the empowerment of young women.

5

Are you on Facebook? Join our cause and donate online! Then invite your friends to do the same.

If you're interested in options two, three, or four, or have another creative option to add, contact Joanne N. Smith, executive director, at jsmith@ggenyc.org

Acknowledgments

Joanne N. Smith

Thank you, Lord—without you none of this would be possible. Conra Gist, I'm so blessed to have you in my life. Thank you for lending us your brilliance and giving me your tireless support. Lorrie Johnson, Ruby Lawrence, Erica Singleton, and Brenda Trinidad, what great friends, you four believed in me at times that I wasn't sure of myself. Farah Tanis, you're a living legend and revolutionary. Thank you for everything. The lineage of gender justice warriors in my family is reflected in matriarchs Therese Lamothe, "Tai Tai," who taught us spiritual connectedness and love beyond our flesh; Ninive Leger, "Maman Ninive," who taught us strategic sacrifice and hard work for the larger vision; and Ernanie Taluy, "Maman Nanie," who taught us kindness and laughter for the soul. My mother Irmone Leger and second mother Marie Claude Joseph continue to show me what it means to be a lifelong learner and spirited warrior, while my wise cousins Guilaine Leger, Najla Florez, and Danielle Leger have shown me time and again what it means to feel the fear and be brave anyway. Natasha Thompson and Rachel Smith, you remain my anchors, irreplaceable sisters in the struggle who have blessed me with my amazing nieces, nephews, cousins, and godchildren, for whom I work to leave this world just a bit safer and a tad more just. To my dad Ralph Smith, brother Everette Thompson, the great men, aunts, and the many loved ones that I haven't mentioned by name, you know that my love for you runs deep. Thank you for all that you've done for me and Girls for Gender Equity. *Ubuntu, I am because we are.*

To my coauthors in the struggle, what a journey we've been through together. Thank you Mandy Van Deven for believing in the power of teen girls to begin Sisters in Strength at GGE, and for bringing your whole self to this work. Meghan Huppuch, you're a kind yet fearless leader. It was a pleasure writing with both of you brilliant women.

Mandy Van Deven

After writing a book about mentoring young women, it is only fitting that I express my admiration for the three women who positively shaped my own upbringing in ways that there is not space enough to name. These inspirational women give me the strength, insight, courage, and support to impact the lives of others. I owe an unending gratitude to my two sisters, Lara Sloan and Dani Humphries, and especially to my mother, Jeani Blalock. We have loved and fought each other fiercely. Growing up in a house of women, I learned how powerful we can all be when we confront a common threat.

Thanks must also be given to those who lift me up when the weight of this heavy work becomes hard to bear: Joel Bordeaux, Dawn Kitto, Devon Claridge, Laura Jankstrom, Brittany Shoot, and Matt Klein. And, of course, this book would never have happened without my two coauthors, colleagues, and friends: Joanne and Meghan. I thank you for continuing to include me in this work and for making every day less of a struggle, not only for me, but for all girls and women.

Meghan Huppuch

Through joyful and challenging times, I remain entirely thankful for the love I receive from those closest to me. Blessing me with unending support, my family is the center I always return to. I am grateful every day for the feminist values instilled in me by my parents, Molly and Bill Huppuch. On my search for myself, I have found, countless times, pieces of each of you; I cherish each and every one. My sisters, Kirsten Fink and Birgit Huppuch, thank you for showing me what it means to be strong, independent women. And lastly, thank you to my partner, Elana Fogel—you are incredibly consistent and kind.

Writing this book alongside Joanne and Mandy has been an intense and fulfilling experience. Thank you, coauthors, for the opportunity and privilege to play a part in Girls for Gender Equity's herstory. It's an honor to work beside you both and have you as mentors and friends.

GIRLS FOR GENDER EQUITY

There is something to be said for the brave ones who submit to a blind leap of faith when they take that first step. Thank you founding board members and volunteers—Terri Clarke, Madeline Curren, Meghan Faux, Mary Ferry, Ravonda Oden, Unson Pak, Starlyn Perkins, Farah Tanis, Marcia Thurmond, Maryellen Waters, Tiffany Wilkins, Sharon Williams—our "mom-and-pop" shop of an organization is scaling up! Thank you to our current board of directors who have faith in our vision, and trust in our collective power.

We have had the pleasure of working with over five hundred interns and volunteers from our three core programs. We offer our gratitude to each of you for showing up strong and sticking with us, especially through unpleasant circumstances: Alicia Ashley, Haleema Ahmed, Katie Barnett, Heather Burack, Sala Cyril, Emily Durant, Man Wah Fong, Askia Foreman, Bryan Mariner, Sherill-Ann Mason, Tal Naveh, Kelvin Oden, Catherina Oerleman, Kevin Park, Sonnia Parkinson, Janely Perez, Ina Solomon, Anna Solomon, and Mark Zugaro, just to name a few. Thank you for stepping up to the plate for our young people and community. Our community-based organizations list is just as full and there's no way we can name them all. Thank you for being solid partners in this journey. Your integrity and practice keep us pushing to be a better, more effective organization.

To Sabrica Barnett, Lisa Covington, Tim Dorsey, Tiffany Dufu, Jill Eisenhard, Tom Ference, Michelle Fine, Conra Gist, Martha Kamber, Khary Lazarre-White, Divina Payne, Benita Rivera, Kim Sabo-Flores, Diana Sands, Cidra Sebastien, Kaajal Shah, Sippio Small, Alvin Starks, Cynthia Steele, Maria Torre, Amy Wagner, Jason Warwin, Susan Wilcox, and the Lead the Way Fellows—you are "the truth." For reasons each of you know, we were blessed to have worked with you, and call you our allies. PAR ally Sarah Zeller-Berkman, you have helped to shape the legacy of GGE with an effortless skill and thoughtfulness that cannot be taught. Watching you share leadership with young people while we moved through this process was a treat. Thank you for helping us to forget we were working. Brett Stoudt, thank you for presenting your amazing work and introducing us to Sarah, as well as to an entire community of revolutionary researchers at CUNY.

Sisters in Strength youth organizers: your inspiration and genius have taught us that young people are an undervalued resource, and one that we must make room for and value if we truly intend to end all forms of oppression. You're the light, Sisters in Strength, keep shining:

2005 Trisha Stafford, Keisha Stafford, Casandra Antoine, Christine Simon, Monephia Brown, Renee Bullard, Ayanna Woods, Jannia Etienne, Kezzie Joseph, Raquel Talavera, Mecca Windley.

2005–2006 Renee Bullard, Ayanna Woods, Jannia Etienne, Kezzie Joseph, Raquel Talavera, Emma Jenkins, Agnes Oniwe, Mecca Windley, Katrina Brown, Fendi Hope, Aliana Lopez, Julie Bennett, Renotti Williams, Tabitha Cadet.

2006–2007 Agnes Oniwe, Alexandra Gonzalez, Ashley Lewis, Emma Jenkins, Fendi Hope, Jazmine Lincoln, Latosha Belton, Mecca Windley, Toccarra Baguma, Ebony Washington.

2007–2008 Agnes Oniwe, Kyla Lino, Nadia Jalil, Tyleisha Lynah, Kayla Andrews, Chime Dolma, Mandie Simonette-Velasco, Veronica Tirado, Shantu Ealy.

2008–2009 Chiamaka Agbasionwe, Veronica Tirado, Kayla Andrews, Shantu Ealy, Marsha Moses, Amanda Simmonds, Ariel Miles, Nefertiti Martin, N'keya Peters, Cyndi Yahyah, Pamela Otibu, Brittany Brathwaite.

2009–2010 Cerilene Small, Wadia John, Kai Walker, Johanel Caceres, Nyocia Edwards, Tawana McNair, Pamela Otibu, Rolandé Fleurival.

2010–2011 Andrenkia Booker, Alicia Wade, Danielle Bouyer, Fahmida Sultana, Miracle Graham, Natasha Adams, Terrin Jones.

Despite the eloquent affirmations of our sisters of INCITE! in their book, *The Revolution Will Not Be Funded: Beyond the Non-Profit Industrial Complex*, we thank the funders and politicians who believe that our revolution should be funded. Many thanks to the individual donors for your generosity and belief in our work.

To the many GGE staff members over the past ten years, thank you for showing us how good people can be in this world. To the ones we can now call friends, Toyia Taylor, your energy and spirit are unmatched. Thank you for being you. Devon Claridge, you're an amazing ally. Thank you for bringing your passion for gender justice to GGE. Vanessa Valenti, your devotion to gender justice has made this world a much better place. Alexis Seeley, Erica Nelson, Kathleen Durst, Nicole Hamilton, Anja Merilainen, Nadira Saunders, and Judy Chicurel, you are brilliant and talented women, and we're so fortunate that you're on our team.

Last, but certainly not least, we want to thank the Feminist Press for presenting GGE with the opportunity to share our work through the gift of this book. Throughout the process the Feminist Press has remained both gracious and supportive, and has continued to remind us of our larger purpose: to share our work. Thank you to Gloria Jacobs, Amy Scholder, Jeanann Pannasch, Drew Stevens, Maryann Jacob Macias, Amita Manghnani, Elizabeth Koke, Sophie Hagen, and the entire Feminist Press crew for everything you've offered us, and all you continue to do for the world.